# GOK WAN

# GOK WAN

## THE BIOGRAPHY

Emily Herbert

JOHN BLAKE

Published by John Blake Publishing Ltd,
3 Bramber Court, 2 Bramber Road,
London W14 9PB, England

www.johnblakepublishing.co.uk

First published in hardback in 2009

ISBN: 978 1 84454 739 5

British Library Cataloguing-in-Publication Data:

A catalogue record for this book is available from the British Library.

Design by www.envydesign.co.uk

Printed in the UK by CPI William Clowes Beccles NR34 7TL

1 3 5 7 9 10 8 6 4 2

Papers used by John Blake Publishing are natural, recyclable products made from
wood grown in sustainable forests. The manufacturing processes conform to the
environmental regulations of the country of origin.

# CONTENTS

# 1
# EAST MEETS WEST

The abuse rang out across the deprived council estate in Leicester, as a group of youths rounded on a tall, overweight teenage boy of mixed Chinese and English blood. It wasn't the first time he had been called 'queer', 'chinky' or 'faggot', and it wouldn't be the last, but the boy refused to be intimidated, turning on the bullies and giving as good as he got. Nonetheless, the taunts stung and their subject was to remember them for many years afterwards, even when he had become one of the most famous and adored men on TV.

Ironically, given that background, the bullied boy was going to become known for the kind way he treated the people around him. But back then, nothing was further from his thoughts. The bullying was non-stop. It was endless, it was vicious and it was cruel. It was also to toughen the young boy up and make him determined to show his detractors he was going to make something of his life. And, several decades on, he has done just that.

*       *       *

On 9 October, 1974, John Tung Shing, a Chinese immigrant living in Leicester, and his English wife Myra were ecstatic. The couple, who had met while working in a takeaway and now been married for years, had just added another baby to their growing brood. In 1969, Myra had given birth to Oilen, and in 1973 to Kwoklyn. Now the baby of the family had arrived, little Ko-Hen Wan, Chinese for Noisy Big City, a name that would prove exceedingly apt when he grew up.

One day he was going to achieve enormous fame as the television stylist Gok Wan, but there was certainly nothing back then that would hint at the glories to come. Little Gok was in for a very rough childhood, and teenage years that would be marred by obesity and self-doubt. But no one had a clue about what the future would hold for any member of the family and at that stage he was simply the adored baby of the family, a little Anglo-Chinese infant with charm and a winning smile.

For John, in particular, it was the fulfilment of a dream. Originally from Hong Kong, he had come to Britain as a teenager from a poverty-stricken background, and although by no means rich now, was settled with a growing family in the west. It was a huge contrast from where he had started out. 'He came to Leicester from a northern Hong Kong village where his mother would still have been catching fish for lunch,' Gok explained. Now John and his wife ran a restaurant, and had built up a stable family life into which the infant Gok had now arrived. They, as their children would also do, had encountered racism and boorishness as a result of their mixed marriage, but the relationship was a strong one. Their family unit would become a haven when, in Gok's childhood years, matters got out of hand.

But now all the family gathered round to coo at the new arrival, and he was a little thing at birth. 'Gok was the weight of a bag of sugar when he was born,' Oilen recalled. 'He was smaller than his first teddy bear. We had to wrap face cloths round his bottom because he was too tiny for the smallest nappies. We called him Babe, and it's stuck, even though by the time he was four or five he was as robust as the rest of us.' In fact, Gok would have to become very robust indeed – and adept at fighting his corner.

It was a very deprived childhood and not at all easy at the time. 'I was born in a trailer park and we grew up on one of the scariest council estates in Leicester,' said Gok – referring to Fosse Road North in Leicester's West End. 'I've been back since for a drive-around and honestly, I didn't want to get out of the car. It's like the front line out there. Mum is a big, apron-wearing Englishwoman, and we were fat, mixed-race kids. We used to get abuse shouted at us all the time.'

Nor was it directed just at the children. 'Mum was once stopped with Oilen and Kwoklyn in the double buggy and told they couldn't possibly be her kids,' Gok said. 'I don't know how we survived, but it made our family an incredibly tight unit.'

It was, in short, blatant racism. No one really knew what to make of the young Gok, as he himself came to understand in later years. 'My family is very, very close,' he said. 'But it was unusual. We lived on a huge council estate and to be mixed race, and not even black/white mixed race – well, it was a huge deal. My parents went through a lot of prejudice.' So did Gok. It was to shape his childhood, casting a huge shadow over his teenage years and shaping his character. Indeed, Gok was so unhappy growing up that he refused a request from the Leicester tourist board to highlight his home city after he had become famous, simply because his childhood had been so difficult there.

Even as a very small child, however, Gok already knew where his interests lay. If Gok is to be believed, it was his mother who was initially responsible for his love of clothes. 'My mum said when I was three I would have to dress myself,' he said. 'I would get into a different outfit to go and pick up my brother and sister from school. I was slightly neurotic about what I was wearing.' Stories abound about the number of times the young Gok would insist on changing his clothes. If he had been wearing one outfit all day, then it had to be changed for the excursion to the school gates. With hindsight, it is not hard to see how Gok ended up with the job he did.

Gok's parents ran their own catering businesses – they still do – and the whole family was expected to get involved.

Gok, however, was adamant that it wasn't a chore, explaining that he started working for his parents when he was about three. 'It wasn't like child labour, though,' he went on. 'My parents have always owned restaurants or takeaways and they worked such long hours that my sister and I wanted to spend time with them when we were young, so we helped them out. I loved it. I love cooking and hospitality. I always think now that if I gave up being a stylist, I'd probably open a restaurant instead.' It was to promote a rather troubled relationship with food, however, as Gok himself was to acknowledge later on.

As so often with the oldest child, it was Gok's sister who braved the challenges first and led the way for her brothers. 'Because the age gap between Oilen and me is quite big, she was going through puberty and adolescence while I was still very much a child,' said Gok. 'She paved the way for me and my brother. She was the only Anglo-Asian at school and she took all those issues on the chin before we even got there.'

But it didn't stop the bullying being visited on her two younger brothers as well. Oilen went on to become a childcare solicitor, sometimes having to deal with some very unpleasant cases, and it's hard not to surmise that difficulties in her own childhood might have contributed to that.

According to Gok, her influence on him was so great as to influence his sexuality, or so he believed at the time. 'When Oilen was going through her New Romantics phase in the 1980s, she said: "I hope you turn out to be gay, because that will make me really cool,"' said Gok. 'Her influence on me was so strong that until I was about 22 I truly believed it was her fault I was gay.'

She also encouraged his love of clothes. 'My real love of fashion came from my older sister Oilen,' said Gok. 'My parents worked in catering so I spent a lot of time with her. She loved Duran Duran, the whole Goth thing and the New Romantics. I loved seeing her getting ready to go out. I loved the idea of her coming back from school and within an hour she'd transformed herself. I used to think "God, you look so cool."'

The two were always very close. 'When I'm trying to remember how I felt about my sister, it's the lilac of her bedroom and the dusty-pink dust jacket of her book *Little Women*,' Gok said. 'One of my earliest memories is of creeping into her bedroom, which I liked so much better than my Superman one, and lying on her bed reading her book, pretending to be her.' He might have been laying it on a bit thick, but it's clear that from an early age, Gok was attracted to feminine things, choosing his sister's room over his brother's (Kwoklyn was to become a martial arts instructor) and remembering the soft, pastel colours. That he ended up in fashion should have been of no surprise to anyone.

The young Gok hero-worshipped his sister but like so many older siblings, she affected to barely acknowledge him. 'She didn't even notice me,' said the adult Gok. 'I can recall the exact stitching on the back of the grey jacket with the lining coming down at the back that she used to wear when

I was nine, yet I was so not in her orbit, she doesn't even remember me being there. I was effeminate and camp, so afraid of people knowing who I was, that I created this character to hide behind. I was straight out of Disney Club. I remember once leaping up and offering to help make sandwiches for her friends, just so I could be part of her clique, and she said: "OK, then. You do it." And they all marched out of the kitchen. Even now, she's the only person in the entire world who can really get to me.'

They have remained close, as Gok has to all his family, with Oilen providing a shoulder to cry on even as an adult. This phenomenally close relationship with his sister, and his mother, too, also goes some way towards explaining Gok's natural rapport with women. He has always been close to them, liked and loved them, been protected by them and felt entirely natural around them. It is no surprise that woman love him so much.

His natural ebullience and strong personality were apparent from a very early age, too. When he was a young child, Gok's parents ran a restaurant (it closed in the 1980s; at the time of writing, they run a fish and chip bar). It was at this restaurant that he first developed the urge to perform. The infant Gok would be dressed up in black tie and brought out to charm the customers, a feat he not only managed perfectly, but which honed the skills he uses on television today.

'The women customers at our parents' restaurant absolutely loved him,' Oilen recalled. 'They made far more fuss of him than me or my other brother. He was really cute. And always incredibly tactile. He just doesn't seem to have any boundaries. Almost the first thing he does when he meets women for the first time is hug them, which makes them feel safe. He learnt that at a very early age. He's like a sponge – he absorbs people's problems – which is why he's so good at what he does.' Indeed, part of Gok's charm is that he is so tactile, while his sexuality means that women don't feel threatened by him. All of the mannerisms that are apparent today were already manifesting themselves while he was still a child.

It wasn't just in his parents' restaurant that Gok would make women feel nurtured and happy. 'At primary school he used to sit next to his teacher and stroke her leg while she read the story,' Oilen continued. 'He's never had a problem saying to someone: "You're adorable". And he means it. He used to tell our Auntie Dawn she was beautiful, and somehow from him it didn't sound cheesy.' It still doesn't – one of the reasons he's become such a success today. It was a remarkable way to behave, however, not purely because he was brought up in repressed British society, but also because as he got older he started to get such a difficult time from other residents on the housing estate. But somehow, although he suffered, it did not make him bitter or any less empathetic to those around him. He retained the many qualities he had as a small child.

It was the solidity of the family background that helped him most, providing a secure base from which to go out to face the rest of the world. 'My parents are so in love,' Gok said, looking back on his childhood. 'Nothing could ever harm them. They were unbelievable: fun and caring and loving and honest and hard-working and slightly twisted sometimes, like all parents, but nothing too hideous, and none of this is sickening because we argue like cat and dog. But we genuinely love each other. If you upset me now, or if I have a panic attack about being famous, I'll call my mum and she'll talk complete crap and it's what I need to hear. Or if I've fallen in love with a boy and he isn't in love with me but we've had sex anyway and I feel terrible, I'll call my sister.' It is an emotional security that endures to this day.

Another factor in Gok's huge rapport with so many women is not just the closeness to his family members, but the fact that the two women themselves were so different. One is high-powered, the other far more of an Earth mother, but Gok established a very close connection to both. Oilen became something of a role model, while Myra provided huge emotional and moral support.

Oilen 'taught me very strong feminist values and groomed me slightly, in a lovely way,' he said. 'Mum is the complete opposite to her: she loves the apron, which makes her a powerful woman in my eyes. She transcends feminism. She does things for my dad because she loves him.' And she had to put up with abuse as well. An English woman married to a Chinese man might not raise many eyebrows these days, but it did when Gok was growing up. Myra had not only to protect her brood but also to look out for herself.

Gok's mother was clearly the foundation stone of the family. Gok refers to her frequently, citing her not just as an inspiration, but also praising her and her personality in her own right. 'She is a bottomless pit of love and is never judgmental of others,' he told one interviewer. 'She easily sees beyond what a person looks like and always taught us when we were growing up that every person has a right to be in the room. She always told us that we could achieve anything and be whoever we wanted to be — as long as we respected other people. I firmly believe that this attitude has been the cornerstone of my success.' It almost certainly was, and as an adult, it informs Gok's approach to how he treats the people around him. He is famously gentler than other great stylists of his age.

However, he was keen to emphasise that Myra also gave him and his siblings space to be themselves. 'That's not to say that she was the type of mother who was constantly up at school fighting our corner; she made us all fiercely independent in the knowledge that she was there in the background if we needed her,' he said. 'Besides, she wasn't around much because she's a real grafter — another quality I think I've inherited from her.' He was going to need it, too. Success did not come overnight — far from it. He would be in the business for the best part of a decade before he finally got his break.

Gok's parents have always worked hard, and he was brought up on the ethos of hard work and endeavour. Despite losing his way slightly in his late teens, it has been part of his personality ever since and his current work schedule is dominated by what he saw in his childhood — hard graft.

Gok never had any doubts about his sexuality, knowing from a very early age that he was gay. 'When I was about six,' he said to a questioner who asked how old he had been when he worked it out. 'I had a crush on a teacher. I lost my virginity far too young to a guy and a girl in the same week. I was socially bullied into sleeping with the girl, but with the guy I really wanted to. Still, I was very confused about it. I didn't have anything to compare it with. When I see kids now, I feel jealous. It's so much easier; everyone has a gay auntie or uncle now.'

While Gok is so open about his sexuality, it is sometimes forgotten he is actually one of the people responsible for changing the climate of opinion. But at the time, his sexuality contributed to his problems. Although not 'out' as such back then, Gok himself has said he was effeminate, and he wasn't the only person to notice it. It was one of the elements involved in the bullying and it didn't make his life easy.

But while he had no doubts about his sexuality, Gok had very mixed feelings about his racial heritage, probably because it was another factor that made him and his siblings stand out from the rest of his surroundings and became one of the main reasons he was so badly abused. In the 1970s and early 1980s British council estates were hotbeds of racial intolerance, and so a mixed-race couple and their offspring were almost guaranteed to have a difficult time.

'It was a very, very rough place,' said Gok. 'It was a hard place to grow up even for people who did blend in. But being overweight, Chinese, effeminate and gay, it was a nightmare. I was called queer, chinky, faggot. The bullying was relentless and horrible, not just for me, but for my brother and sister as well.'

Perhaps partly as a result of the stress it caused, Gok first developed a nicotine habit when he was very young – one he retains to this day. He was 11 when his father left a cigarette burning in an ashtray and he tried it out himself. 'I thought it was so lovely,' said Gok. 'I nicked a whole packet off him the next week.' Gok, not an academic child, would play truant with some of the local girls and smoke with them in the woods near his home. It was a rare moment of let-up from the problems he was experiencing from the other boys who lived on the estate.

Matters did not ease up as Gok got older. Instead he became an even more obvious target as he gained a huge amount of weight, helped by his parents' choice of profession. Always a slightly chubby little boy, Gok ballooned to an obese 21 stone in his teenage years – almost unrecognisable from the slim figure he cuts today. He knew why, too. 'Our relationship with food was, "If it makes you feel better then eat it," which resulted in three fat, mixed-race kids,' he observed of the growing-up years. 'So life was in many ways difficult. But with her as a mother it never felt too bad.'

Gok's personality was undergoing some sort of

metamorphosis as well: he was developing a loud, brash persona, partly to deflect attention from his weight and partly to live up to it. It affected him, too. Now seriously overweight, he adopted a persona that was quite unlike the one on show today. He went through periods of not being close to his family, denying his racial inheritance, and feeling alienated from everything around him. 'I was quite a tearaway, an angry child,' he said. 'I struggled a lot with my identity.'

But although it would not have seemed so at the time, this was building Gok up for the future. Many highly successful people go through extremely difficult childhoods, including being bullied, and emerge determined to prove themselves to the world. All the resentment he felt at the treatment he was receiving and the determination to stand up for himself would one day going stand him in good stead, while his sheer determination not to give in to the bullies would translate into a determination to make something of his life. But if this agonising period was ultimately going to be the making of him, Gok certainly couldn't see that yet.

There were a few consolations in the difficult life he was leading, however. As he grew older, his love of clothes began to develop – something that would hardly have endeared him to the bullies either – and he was beginning to realise how important they could be. Far more than simply something to keep you from the cold and rain, they could provide a key to the way people behaved around you – a lesson that one day was going to stand Gok in spectacularly good stead.

'At 13, I'd discovered that clothes can change the way people see you,' Gok said. 'I used to be in a tracksuit all the time, but then I went out and got chinos and brogues, so I didn't look like a fat person. I was confident about being big, and I worried that if I got smaller, I wouldn't have the right personality.' In fact, when he lost weight, not only would he keep the personality, he discovered he preferred the way people treated him. But at the time, the persona he'd created was something to hide behind.

The bullying continued but Gok's experiences also made him more resilient and determined to make something of his life. 'Being camp, overweight and Chinese on a council estate in the Midlands was tough,' he said, with some understatement in later years. 'When I was little I saw my brother being bullied, although he's not camp like me and I'd stand up for him. From a very young age I knew bullying could happen and when it did, I handled it in my own way. I became quite mouthy and obnoxious. We just dealt with it. Anybody that goes through any kind of social torment has to. But I come from a strong family who supported me and really were my wall of defence.'

Gok wasn't just fat: he was getting taller and taller, and this just served to make him stand out even more. There seemed to be nothing he could do about his predicament: his height and obesity, married to his Chinese looks, would have made him stand out anywhere (including China) so a Leicester council estate was a parlous place to be.

Even as an adult, Gok has sometimes come across as being

in denial about the racial nastiness of it all. The bullying, according one interview, was not racially based, and he did not use his ethnic roots as a way of fighting back. 'I couldn't do that as a Chinese person; I had to do that as a working-class white person,' he said. 'I was never attacked for being Chinese; I was attacked more for my sexuality and my size.'

What was more likely was that Gok had still not quite come to terms with his Chinese ancestry and so couldn't accept that it was the reason he was having such a difficult time. And then there was the campness, a further personality trait to pick on.

His sister Oilen recalled it slightly differently. 'I was so absorbed with myself as a teenager, my memories of him are pretty sketchy,' she confessed. 'He was bullied a lot, because he was camp, chubby, mixed-race. Poor Babe. It wasn't easy. We were all picked on, but our family was so strong that even when I was getting called half-breed I never wanted to be anything but mixed-race. I was into my books, Babe was always interested in clothes. As a child he'd change five times a day. Years before David Beckham wore a sarong, Gok was wearing one to a club in Leicester with a holey mohair jumper. I remember saying to him: "Promise me you'll get a taxi right to the door."'

Gok might have been in denial about the bullying having anything to do with his Chinese roots because for many years, he was actually in denial about the roots themselves. Although it is patently obvious, looking at him, that he has Asian blood, as a child he placed himself very much in the context of the country he was growing up in, not the one his father had left behind. This might have been a question of survival – he wanted to emphasise what he had in common with other people in the area, not that which made him different, so much so that he barely even felt Chinese.

Indeed, this lasted right into adulthood. In an interview given when he was 34, he said of feeling Chinese, 'It's a new thing, actually. For years I stopped myself being Chinese. When I was growing up, we were the only Asian family in our area – can you imagine? But, had I not been bullied to within an inch of my life, had I not stood up for myself at 13 and said, "Right, you fuckers," I wouldn't be doing what I am now.'

He was right. Gok was going to be moving into the world of television, a notoriously tough environment and he needed to be tough. He also needed to be able to rise above the travails that might otherwise have destroyed him. Above all, he needed to accept the fact that he was half-Chinese. Without that, he would never be able to feel comfortable in his own skin, and never ultimately know who he really is.

It is no coincidence that as Gok has become increasingly successful, he's increasingly in tune with his Chinese roots, not least because in the world he was going to enter, having an exotic background is no barrier at all to success. Indeed, it is positively welcome. It's only in places where it made Gok feel unusual and uncomfortable that having a Chinese heritage seemed to be a burden to bear.

Strangely, Gok actually knew far more about his father's

side of the family than he did his mother's. 'My dad's from Hong Kong and has very strong genes, so we all look Chinese,' he told one interviewer, 'but my mum's English and though she never knew her father, we know he was really tall – hence my height. It's pretty bizarre for a Chinese guy to be six feet one.'

But if that which doesn't destroy you makes you stronger, then Gok was gaining in strength, little did he know it. He was already displaying another trait that would stand him in good stead in later years: steadfastly making himself the centre of attention. It might have been for all the wrong reasons, and the attention he was summoning might have been almost wholly negative, but as an adult he was going to be able to do the same thing to considerably better effect.

Gok might have loved fashion, but at that stage he didn't see it as the way ahead, even though school certainly wasn't going to provide him with a way out of his difficult life. Unlike his elder sister, Gok was not in the slightest bit academic and had no idea what he wanted to do. He was filled with resentment about the way people were talking to him, on top of which there seemed no obvious career path for him to take. 'I was quite an angry child and I left school very young – before I had sat GCSEs,' he later recalled. 'I didn't have any direction, really. I thought I might want to be a farmer, but that was only because they look sexy in wellies. Then I thought about archaeology because it sounded important. I had no idea what an archaeologist actually did.'

One obvious step would have been to follow his parents

into catering, but Gok did not appear to want that. To this day he talks about opening a restaurant, but it's clear that fashion really is his life. However, at that stage, it wouldn't have occurred to anyone that Gok might forge the kind of career he did do – he was, after all, a working class boy from a very rough council estate.

In retrospect, it's not difficult to understand the choice that Gok actually made. Large, camp and theatrical, accustomed to performing for customers from an early age and effortlessly commanding attention from everyone he encountered, the surprise would have been if Gok hadn't made the choice he did. He wanted to shape a new life and get out of Leicester. So he decided to take to the stage.

# 2
# A BUTTERFLY EMERGES FROM THE CHRYSALIS

At first sight, it looks like a brilliant idea – inspired, even. Gok was clearly not turning out to be the sort of person who would have a job in an office, so a career on the boards seemed an obvious choice to make. Even now, watching Gok flitting across the television screens it's possible to imagine him in dramatic roles. It wasn't long, however, before Gok discovered that it was not going to be ideal, either.

Initially, Gok obtained a diploma in performing arts at the Charles Keene College of Further Education in Leicester. 'I wanted to be on stage,' he said. 'I was obsessed with the idea of putting on a character and hiding myself.' This was, in many ways, what he'd been doing for years: he'd been hiding behind the weight, the bombastic personality, the sheer force that was not quite the real Gok. And he'd been doing it so successfully, there seemed no reason he wouldn't be able to transfer this talent to the stage as well. What had he been doing as a teenager if not acting all along? And now it seemed he was going to make a career of it. It was a logical move, in many ways.

From there Gok went to the Central School of Speech and Drama in North London, where his dreams soon crashed and burned. New to living in London, Gok might have been relieved to get away from Leicester, but it was still familiar and it was his home. But this was an alien city, 'the big smoke', and he soon discovered that he was on a course he hated. Ironically, he would soon fit into London life far more easily than he ever did in Leicester, but for now it was miserable and bringing him down. He was lonely, he didn't fit in and it all felt as if it was going wrong.

The problem was quite simple: Gok discovered he couldn't act. Worse still, he still felt cut off from everyone around him. They took their acting very seriously indeed, in a way that Gok certainly didn't, and coming from smart backgrounds they (whisper it) looked down on him for being working class. The course was an unmitigated disaster, and left Gok feeling worse than he had done before he left home. To this day he remains convinced that he was accepted only because it suited the school, rather than any innate talent that he might have possessed. 'Ticking boxes for public funding is what I call it,' he said. 'Chinese, fat, gay: I'd got in for the wrong reasons. I was a regurgitated product of Thatcher. My parents were uneducated, I'd never written an essay in my life, but I was told: "Yes, you can do this" — and I couldn't! Ooh, shit!'

Rarely for Gok, he went on to display some bitterness at the behaviour of the college by raising expectations in him that could not be fulfilled. 'You did me no good by telling me I could!' he went on. 'It was awful. I missed my family and friends and I was landed in white middle-class hell. I was literally surrounded by double-barrelled names and Porsches. They walked the walk [i.e. they pretended to be all street and cool] but then dad's helicopter would arrive to take them shopping in New York for the weekend, and I was in a bedsit, trying to get a job in a takeaway.'

It was an experience he referred back to again and again after he'd found fame. This was the first time he had encountered people who considered themselves to be full-on intellectuals (whether they really were is a different matter), which made him feel yet more insecure. 'I felt like "Gok from the Block",' he said on another occasion. 'I felt like everyone around me was talking non-stop about [German playwright Bertold] Brecht and [Russian director Constantin] Stanislavsky. I didn't know how to join in. At Central it's all pretty serious, but my talent was for making people laugh and I loved the West End. I know it's cheesy, but I love a good sing-song and I think if I had gone somewhere a bit more "jazz bands", maybe I would never have become a stylist.'

It was a hideous time: going from being bullied in Leicester to being patronised in London, with still no obvious route for him to take, was driving him to despair. But what was the alternative? Gok would barely have been aware that the job of stylist existed at that stage, although he was going to come across it soon enough.

Finally he dropped out. 'As with everything I've ever done, I let my confidence and sense of humour carry me through for a while,' said Gok. 'But there comes a point when you need the talent to back it up and I had to admit I just didn't have it. [But] I was gutted to be leaving drama school. Acting had inspired me to sort my life out and I was scared to leave it behind.'

Ultimately, it was probably inevitable that he would have had to leave. Academic institutions and Gok just didn't mix. 'I had always found school and college stifling,' he confessed. 'I'm not good at being marked or taking exams.' As it turned out, it was the best thing he could have done, but at the time, it felt like just another failure. And for a boy who was so close to his family to go through all this without them – although emotionally he was as close to them as he had ever been – made it harder still to bear.

But it was around this period that the Gok of today began to appear. When he went up to drama school, he still weighed 21 stone, which could not have helped matters, but that perhaps provided the impetus for change. Gok had begun to realise that he was not happy with the weight and wanted to lose it but, initially at least, he had no idea how that was to be done. 'I went on a diet when I first went to drama school and I ate an entire bag of dry pasta with two cans of tuna and a whole tub of mayonnaise – I thought that was a healthy meal because it wasn't deep-fried or served with chips,' he said. 'I was really uneducated about food, but I found out more about it.'

Food had become an addiction by this point, and like many addicts, Gok was nervous about turning into a different person from the one he'd become. Not, by his telling of it, that the person he presented to the outside world back then had much to do with the reality. 'In fact, I was more uncomfortable about losing the weight, which I did when I was 20,' he recalled to one questioner, who'd asked him about coming out. 'I'd built up this personality. It wasn't really Gok. It was a loud, brash, camp person to match the physicality.'

In truth, both the weight and the personality had become a kind of defence mechanism. Both held people at bay: they were the way by which Gok didn't allow himself to get hurt. Losing weight and toning it down meant more than just changing his appearance and behaviour: it also made Gok more vulnerable to the outside world. There is psychological safety in sticking to long-held habits, such as overeating. Change, on the other hand, can open up a whole new world and for someone who's already feeling insecure, this can be very hard to bear.

Once he'd begun, it took Gok about a year to lose all the weight. 'It was a competitive thing,' he said. 'I just decided. It was ridiculous crash-dieting: it was the totally wrong way of doing it but it worked.' It also made him realise there was a different world out there and that, having totally changed his appearance, it was going to treat him differently, too. 'You know, if you're a fat kid, half-Chinese and gay, you are treated completely differently to how you are if you're 11 stone, like I am now,' he said in an interview in 2008. And carrying all that weight for so long was going to make him the ideal person for women to confide in about their insecurities about their own appearance: they could trust him because he'd been in exactly the same position.

Meanwhile, some good did come out of his time at drama school, even if Gok wouldn't quite realise it yet. He had always been obsessed with clothes and as a trainee actor, he began to learn about the importance of costumes and appearance. 'If you give an actor the wrong character, you misrepresent their character and it might take an hour or two of dialogue to undo that first impression,' he explained. 'The same principle applies to real life. Whether I'm dressing ordinary people or pop stars, I'm giving them an image to project.' It was perhaps the most important lesson he learnt at the time and one that was going to remain with him for many years. Indeed, it was the making of his career.

Slowly but surely, however, Gok was beginning to find his way. He was in London now, with all the opportunities the capital could afford him, and he was going to do what it took to get on in life. In retrospect it's quite clear new avenues were opening up, but Gok had to find out where they were. All he could see back then were dead ends.

'I bummed around for a little while,' Gok said of his time after drama school. Asked how he got into fashion, he continued, 'It was completely by accident, really. I just floated from rubbish job to rubbish job, with no self-esteem and no idea what I wanted to do. Then I went into hair and make-up. I was a session hair-and-make-up artist, and I learned on the job, really. I started working with a fashion stylist and loved what she did, and that kind of inspired me to do it myself. It was all by chance.'

But it was more than that. Gok came from a hard-working background and he soon began to show the hard graft that had kept his parents going throughout their lives. Fashion is a very tough industry to break into: low pay, long hours and unbelievable competition. But Gok stuck to his guns. 'I come from a working-class background where there were not many opportunities and you had to create opportunities for yourself,' he said. 'Me and my brother were brought up in this kind of environment and we've all done well for ourselves. Go, Team Gok! I'm a firm believer that drive, initiative and motivation are just as important as which university you manage to get into.'

Many years later, when he was a big name in the fashion industry, he returned to the theme time and time again. 'I'm definitely not knocking education, but it isn't just about which university or school you go to,' he said. 'When I'm looking for a new assistant, I don't even bother looking at their credentials or which course they've done. It's not that I'm saying it's not a stepping stone to getting where you want to be, I just hate the idea that children leave school thinking they have to go to university and get a first degree if they want to get anywhere in life. I think it's important for them to know there is more than one route – there are other options out there.'

Indeed, so convinced of this was he that Gok went on to develop rather an unusual way of measuring the people he was to work with. 'The first thing I get them to do for me is clean my flat,' he declared. 'Not because I'm being pretentious or precious – it's because it's a really good way of finding out about that person's sense of style as well as picking up on other skills they might have from the way they arrange things.'

In short, he was searching for a person's innate sense of what looks right. 'You can teach people to sew, to set up a fashion shoot, send emails, deal with the media, but what you can't teach is a sense of style,' Gok continued. 'You've either got it or you haven't – it's as simple as that. By getting them to arrange my flat I get a really good idea about their individual sense of style.'

But all that was to come. Back when he'd just dropped out of drama school, Gok was only beginning to learn his trade in the fashion industry while subsisting on less than nothing in one of the most expensive cities in the world. He would never have imagined that one day he was going to be in a position to choose his own assistants, let alone be getting them to clean his flat. In fact, his first job was working for Habitat: 'I rocked up to work at Habitat years ago in head-to-toe beige,' he recalled. 'I looked like an artificial limb.' As for the job itself, it was not a great success. 'I was terrible,' declared Gok.

But he had at least made a start. The little boy who'd been obsessed with fashion had grown into a young man who not only loved clothes, but knew what to do with them – and not only on himself. Equally importantly, he also loved women, and he was going to be able to combine those two loves to spectacular effect. He was also fortunate in that he was going to be able to learn his trade out of the limelight: it was only when he was good and ready that Gok was going to finally take centre stage.

Something else was happening back then, too, although Gok could not have known it would have anything to do with him. Television was changing: reality shows were emerging and a couple who had started out before him were leading their way into a territory that had not been fully explored. It was going to be remarkably fruitful, not just for them, but for a great many people who came after them. Seeds were taking root that would one day grow into huge trees.

In brief, two rather plummy journalists, Susannah Constantine and Trinny Woodall, had started writing a column called 'Ready to Wear' in the *Daily Telegraph* in 1994. The idea was that women could look good whatever their shape, and do so using clothes from the high street, not a designer shop that was beyond most people's financial reach. The girls – bossy, opinionated and posh – had already got quite a following and they were attracting an increasing amount of attention.

A book, *Ready 2 Dress*, and a dot-com business, ready2shop.com, followed, and although neither was successful, the duo were very much rising stars. While there had always been stylists, they had never been quite like these two, and the potential for them, and for the genre of television they would go on to front, was huge. Soon they were to be commissioned to present their very own television series, which was to prove a spectacular triumph. It was the start of the obsession with the makeover show.

No one realised at that point quite what a phenomenon it would prove. The timing, however, was perfect: a combination of the growth of reality television when women were becoming obsessed with their bodies as never before, while at the same time they had more money than ever to do something about it. It provided all the ingredients Trinny and Susannah — and Gok after them — needed to become a success.

Of course, Gok had no inkling this new phenomenom would one day be the making of him. He continued to flit from job to job, searching for what was going to be right for him, but all the while gaining knowledge and learning more and more about how to style someone's looks. He was slowly but surely making contacts, and as his own body shape was changing, he was gaining confidence in the new slimline Gok. He was beginning to see how differently people treated him when he was slim and fashionable from when he was obese and slightly threatening, and it was a change he liked.

Meanwhile, in the background, Gok's family remained as supportive as ever. They might all be in Leicester while he was in London, but the close emotional ties between all of them grew stronger by the year. Gok, the baby of the family, was out on his own now, but he still had his parents and siblings to support him, and knew he could call on them in his hour of need. But that hour of need was receding now, because fate had great things in store. Little did he know it, but in about a decade hence, Gok was going to be one of the best known and much loved faces on TV.

# 3
# REALITY BITES

**W**hen the definitive book of unexpected consequences comes to be written, perhaps one of the oddest entries will be that involving the 1988 Writers Guild of America strike, a TV show called *COPS* and Gok Wan. But there is a direct link between the three. While Gok was still a surly, fat teenager with attitude in Leicester, events were going on across the pond that would have a direct effect on his future. Back in the late 1980s, there was no such thing as a television stylist, certainly not in the sense that we think of it today, but it was then that the train of events was set in motion that led to Gok's future success.

Indeed, that writers' strike was to change the face of television, little did anyone know it at the time. Contrary to popular belief, there had been some form of reality television stretching back through the decades, with perhaps the most well known being Granada Television's *Seven Up*, a documentary series following the development of seven-year-old children from different socio-economic backgrounds, which began in 1964. But the explosion in today's reality shows goes straight back to the events in 1988.

To put it bluntly, with all the scriptwriters on strike, there was nothing to put on air because nothing was getting written. So it was the future producers of reality television's great good luck that a producer called John Langley, who had gone on raids with drug enforcement officers for a series of programmes about drugs, had a novel idea. Why not make a programme following the police in their work and at home? This had never been done at any length before: putting real life people in real life situations on prime time television. Along with his producing partner Malcolm Barbour, Langley pitched the idea to Stephen Chao, an executive at Fox.

A less far-sighted man than Chao might have rejected the idea without a second glance. But the pitch had quite a lot going for it at a time when the writers were striking. It was exactly what was needed: it required no script, no actors, no music, no planning and none of the standard paraphernalia required to make a television show. If timing is everything, then this timing could not have been more right. The writers had shot themselves in the foot: they had caused the creation of a new type of television that didn't need them – and they had paved the way for people like Gok.

On 11 March, 1989, the first episode of *COPS* came out. It was totally revolutionary. The producers had dropped the idea of following the policemen home in favour of concentrating on their work, but this was more than enough to grip the viewers. What you saw really was what you got: the policemen and their work were portrayed without any editorial voiceover: their actions spoke entirely for themselves. It caused an immediate and lasting sensation, proving once and for all that the ordinary Joe in the street could be as fascinating on the small screen as any highly paid actor. This was television showing real life.

The series, which airs to this day, has been a spectacular success. The first episode featured the work of the Sheriff's Office of Broward County in Florida, and locations all across the United States have appeared in the series. The people who actually make the programme have sometimes had to get involved: on one occasion a sound mixer had to help a police officer perform CPR (resuscitation after a heart attack). On another, a cameraman (who was also a Las Vegas reserve police officer) had to drop his camera and help another officer wrestle with a suspect. His camera was picked up by the soundman, who went on filming the scene. Viewers loved it and television executives realised they had a format that could make them a fortune. Other versions have since been filmed in London, Hong Kong and Russia.

Of course, *COPS* as a programme bears no similarity whatsoever with *How to Look Good Naked*, but it was the start of what would one day become a massive trend. A long way from the glossy production techniques associated with so much of 1980s television (such as *Dallas* and *Dynasty*), *COPS* came across as some kind of cinema verité. It introduced the viewing public to a totally different kind of viewing than anything they had seen before, and was eventually to make stars out of the unlikeliest of people, including, of course, Gok Wan. Reality television still provokes a curled lip in some quarters, and there are clearly some programmes that have not entirely been thought through, but the public clearly adores shows like Gok's.

That, however, was still to come. After the United States had led the way, it was Holland that took up the baton, with a series called *Number 28*. This was in many ways a foreshadowing of *Big Brother*, yet it ran for only one season. Named after the house in which it was filmed, *Number 28* took seven complete strangers, all students, and followed their lives for several months. It debuted in 1991, but unlike the programmes that were to follow it, the strangers were not kept in isolation and were not set tasks. It didn't set the world on fire, but it was to prove hugely influential. It aired when Gok was still living in Leicester, and although he didn't see it, it was to shape forces that had an enormous impact on his life.

It might not have lasted that long, but someone took notice, namely, MTV, which devised a similar format that went on to become a hit. In 1992 another show that runs to this day premiered: *The Real World*, in which seven strangers moved into a house together and were filmed inter-reacting, as well having their adventures in the outside world put on the screen. The show's producers, Mary-Ellis Bunim and

Jonathan Murray, originally toyed with the idea of some kind of pre-scripted format, but eventually dropped this in favour of allowing the participants to behave totally naturally.

The people involved were 18-25, mirroring the age of the audience they were looking for, and, foreshadowing *Big Brother* nearly a decade later, the house was furnished with a pool table and Jacuzzi. It also contained a fish tank – a metaphor for the show. Shades of *Big Brother* also arose through the use of the 'confessional', a soundproof room into which the cast were invited once a week, individually, to talk about their experiences of being on the show. It was another sensation and another step along the road of reality television: traditional viewing was changing beyond anything anyone could have imagined before.

The programme made a huge impact in the United States, and quite a few of the participants went on to become stars in their own right. (One, Kevin Powell, was a candidate for the US House of Representatives – Gok, take note.) The third season, set in San Francisco, made particular waves as it contained the AIDS activist Pedro Zamora. This generated huge publicity about the plight of men living with AIDS, and after his death in November 1994, just after the series ended, he was praised publicly by President Bill Clinton. Zamora had made one friend in particular during his time in the house: Judd Winick, who became a comic-book writer and penned the graphic novel *Pedro and Me*. It was also this series that revealed for the first time the true full potential of reality TV. Earlier participants had not become public figures who stayed in the headlines even after their time on screen had ended: now they did. More important still, viewers couldn't get enough of it. People began to realise that not just this format but any number of other reality programmes could have a huge impact if they were shown on TV.

The changing face of technology also made this kind of programme possible on a widespread basis. The television commentator Charlie Brooker said that it was only because of the invention of computer-based, non-linear editing systems that it could be done. This meant that hours and hours of footage could be edited down very quickly, something that had not been possible before. But attitudes were changing, too. Purists might not have liked it, but this was a very democratic way of running television. Ordinary people were becoming its stars.

It was not until 1996 that British television finally woke up to the mainstream possibilities of reality television, although when it did so, it was an astounding success. The first of what can really be called the modern generation of British reality TV shows was a makeover programme, although it was very different from the ones Gok would go on to present. It was *Changing Rooms*, a show that inspired innumerable successors and fuelled a DIY boom.

The show, originally hosted by Carol Smillie and 'Handy' Andy Kane, used a format that had two couples swapping houses and then doing up the other's property. It was bound to cause ructions and frequently did. There were more revelations for the programme-makers: it made very good television, provoking reactions from the public, who were either pleased or appalled by what they saw. The stars were important, but so were the participants, something Trinny and Susannah certainly cottoned on to, although in the end they might have gone too far. That was something Gok was to grasp with greater success, for unlike his two posh predecessors, he coaxed reactions out of people by using kindness. He became the face of reality television using gentleness, not strife.

Many of the designers who took part in *Changing Rooms* went on to become household names, including Linda Barker, Laurence Llewelyn-Bowen and Anna Ryder Richardson, all of whom had careers that extended far beyond the remit of the show. The programme also had its fair share of disasters, which also made for riveting viewing. On one occasion Linda Barker designed a room to house a valuable collection of teapots: the shelves collapsed, destroying them.

Laurence Llewelyn-Bowen was probably the most controversial in his designs: his modernism-meets-Versailles rooms did not always meet with their owners' approval and provoked strong reactions, which also made excellent viewing. And on one memorable occasion, Anna Ryder Richardson decorated a room by placing undergarments in frames on the wall: 'Why should I want this shit in my room? I've got children!' shrieked the owner, before bursting into tears. But it all made great telly and the viewers loved it. Viewing figures soared: the producers had a hit on their hands.

As well as inspiring other home makeover shows in the UK, *Changing Rooms* gave rise to various overseas versions, including *Trading Spaces* in the United States. The original British version became cult viewing across the pond, too, featuring in the 'Lights, Camera, Relationship' episode of *Sex and the City*. By the time it came to the end of its last run in 2004, it had become an institution of sorts – and an example of what a really good makeover format could be. It was hugely influential in the number of programmes it inspired, and it's not putting it too strongly to say that it changed the shape of British television. It was a revelation to everyone involved.

By the turn of the new century, reality television had become a staple of television life. Quite apart from the huge, albeit now diminishing impact of *Big Brother*, first shown in 2000, there are now whole channels that are devoted to reality telly: *Zone Reality* in the UK, and *Fox Reality* in the United States. But it was on 29 November, 2001, when the kind of show that was to make Gok a star finally came in to being: Trinny and Susannah first appeared in *What Not to Wear* on BBC2. A new type of television sensation was born.

The idea couldn't have been simpler: take someone who was frumpy and give them a fashion makeover, proving that there are clothes for every shape. Specifically, participants (nominated by family or friends as being particularly unfashionable) were ambushed by our two heroines and, having received advice, given £2,000 to spend on new clothes. Both girls were happy to manhandle their subjects, and it was not unknown for a contestant to be reduced to tears. The public loved it, and the presenters: two rather bullying posh girls, who were not afraid to tell it like it is. By the show's second run they were managing to get celebrities to appear, including Jeremy Clarkson, who memorably remarked, 'I'd rather eat my own hair than shop with these two again.'

The duo, with their glitzy backgrounds – Trinny came from a rich family and Susannah had dated Viscount Linley in her youth – became unlikely folk heroes, but back then, at least, the public loved them. And a lot of what they said was sound common sense. The show received critical acclaim and the industry lauded them too: in 2002 Trinny and Susannah won a Royal Television Society Award for best factual presenters. The next year they did a spin-off called *What Not to Wear on the Red Carpet*; their celebrity guests were Jo Brand and Sophie Raworth.

The following year they climbed to greater heights still. Now on the verge of becoming national treasures (although some people loathed them for their perceived cruelty – Trinny and Tranny was one of the kinder nicknames they attracted), their show was switched to BBC1. The initial series of *What Not to Wear* had lasted 30 minutes with one subject; now it was extended to a full hour, with two. In later series, it was no longer family and friends that did the nominating: the would-be subjects themselves sent in videos, saying why they felt they should feature on the show. The manhandling continued, as did the blunt, tell-it-like-it-is advice.

The series continued to be extremely popular. More celebrities were enticed on screen: Trish Goddard, David Baddiel and Ingrid Tarrant all appeared. In 2005, none other than Britney Spears announced she was a fan: 'The girls are so dramatic in the makeovers, you just get caught up in it,' she remarked. 'Would I go on the show? Never say never.' In fact, as well as spawning international version, the English show has been seen all over the world, and is regularly repeated on UK Style. At the time it seemed as if the girls were invincible: certainly no one would have thought that a half-English, half-Chinese man who towered over them and came from a rough council estate in Leicester would ever take their crown.

Proof, if it were needed, that Trinny and Susannah had made it big came when Alistair McGowan and Ronni Ancona took to spoofing them on their own show, *Big Impression*. Meanwhile, they gained the ultimate seal of approval from the children of the world when they appeared as two killer androids, Trinn-e and Zu-Zanna in an episode of *Dr Who* ('Bad Wolf'). There was also an appearance on *Children in Need* in 2004, giving Little Mo and Mo Harris from *EastEnders* makeovers: they seemed to be on a roll.

With the benefit of hindsight, it is possible to see that Trinny and Susannah made the wrong move. They left the show that had made them famous, handing over to Lisa

Butcher and Mica Paris, who might not have made the same impact but proved to be a safe pair of hands, and moving across to ITV to make *Trinny and Susannah Undress the Nation*. But there was an immediate problem, in that they weren't allowed to take their successful format across with them, so they had to devise another way to show people how to dress.

The solution they came up with was to find couples who were having problems in their relationships, and who could use clothes as a means of solving them. This immediately, and understandably, caused comments to the effect they were stylists and journalists, not relationship counsellors. Nonetheless, the show started off well, and its presenters were made the faces of Littlewoods Direct shopping. Orders rose by 30 per cent. But they were not the first to leave a successful format and discover that their brand didn't travel: their initial viewing figures were not to last.

But at the time, Trinny and Susannah were on a roll. The girls were nothing if not game: they advertised the new show by posing naked, covering themselves only with their hands. The public loved it, but it was quite clear from the start that this was a very different kind of programme from *What Not to Wear*, and that the brashness and bullying that had gone with the former was perhaps not so appropriate here.

The format was this: the girls met a couple having relationship difficulties, talked to them about their problems and then asked them to put on the clothes in which they felt most comfortable. Dinner with friends and family followed, wearing these clothes. The next day the couple had to view each other naked (the girls saw them only in silhouette from behind a screen), point out their partner's best bits, and the girls then took them shopping separately. A full makeover followed, and voila! Everyone was happy again.

It was hardly surprising the show raised eyebrows from the start. The first episode featured a couple, Ellie and Lester, whose problems looked rather more serious than anything that could be solved by a few new clothes. Lester was 19 years older than Ellie and seven inches shorter; aged 53, he stayed at home to look after the couple's two autistic sons. Ellie, meanwhile, confessed to an affair. They were subjected to the Trinny and Susannah treatment, but ultimately, viewers were left feeling they might have needed help of a very different sort. This appeared to be trivialising people's problems, and they were quite serious problems. Could a change of clothes really signal a change of life?

Ironically, when Gok hit the television screens a few years later, he did what Trinny and Susannah had tried, but with much greater success. His subjects also needed a boost of confidence to change deep-rooted fears and problems, but possibly because his style was so different, it actually appeared to work.

Trinny and Susannah, however, seemed to take a rather more brusque approach, and the people they featured continued to have problems that needed a very different kind of help. And so it went on, and as it did so, ratings began to fall. The second series didn't attract nearly as many viewers, and by the time they embarked on *Trinny and Susannah*

*Undress the Nation* at the end of 2007, their star was clearly on the wane. But the television makeover show was as popular as ever — it was merely that the two women had begun to grate, and had not managed to find a format that matched the popularity of their original series. The viewers were switching off.

In fact, the two really were perceived now to be going too far. Upper-class bossiness was one thing, but some people thought their barbs were really becoming too sharp. What had initially seemed straightforward common sense was beginning to feel a bit mean, and with some of the people they spoke to clearly rather vulnerable, a more gentle approach was now on the cards. But Trinny and Susannah didn't do gentle, not by a long shot, and had been developing their particular style for so long now that changing would have been quite a break. Criticism was growing, and there were signs that the tide was beginning to turn.

And so the scene was set for someone who would compliment women rather than criticise, who would make them feel good about themselves, while pointing them in the direction of self-improvement. A completely new type of person was needed, someone so different from Trinny and Susannah that a whole new way of doing makeover shows was to be presented to the nation. And television was about to find just that.

\*     \*     \*

In the early 1990s, however, Gok was a long way from becoming that star. For a start, he was still losing all that weight, and it was clear where the problem stemmed from, as Gok himself acknowledged. His parents were caterers and their whole life revolved around food, which was not conducive to keeping weight down. 'If you go round to their house, within minutes, food is either happening or being discussed,' he said. 'When they had the restaurant, they'd come home from work at midnight and cook fried rice and steak — we'd smell it coming up the stairs, then we'd all get up and eat it at 2am. When a woman says to me, "I cannot bear the thought of anyone seeing me naked," I know how that feels.'

He was being sensible, though, about getting the weight off. 'Lifestyle changes and a decision to eat less,' he said, when asked how he'd done it. 'I started walking more, taking the stairs not the lift, that sort of thing. I also reduced the food I ate and educated myself about what was good for me.'

But now that he was living in London, he was finding a far healthier relationship with food. He also decided it was time to declare to his family that he was gay. 'I came out to Oilen first,' Gok revealed. 'She said she always knew, but then it was hard to miss. She did what Oilen always does: she told me how I felt. She said, "You'll feel better when you tell Mum and Dad." When I phoned Mum, she said, "It's OK. Oilen told me." Dad was brilliant. He didn't say anything, but when I first took a boyfriend home, he made up a bed in the lounge.'

Indeed, Gok was aware that this was potentially a very problematic area for his father. 'Dad was amazing,' he said. 'In the Chinese community, views on homosexuality are pretty much where everyone else's were in the 1970s: they're 30 years behind, and I don't think that's about to change. When Mum [told] me she knew, I was devastated. I was so scared of losing them. It was a very, very, very big moment in my life.'

It is for many gay men, of course, but Gok was in a particularly difficult position. Being mixed race and coming from a rough council estate, Gok had already encountered quite enough problems as it was: having to out himself to a conservative family was not easy. But their complete acceptance of his news and of their son being who he was made it much easier for him in the longer term. Gok has certainly never made any pretence of being anything but gay once his television career began, and his parents' early attitude must have influenced that.

One interviewer asked whether having the truth out in the open was a relief. 'I don't remember,' Gok replied. 'I've blocked that one out. It's weird, isn't it? I'm still dealing with my sexuality, I think. But they're cool about my boyfriends. They've stayed at the house. My parents went through so much themselves, I think that's allowed them to be more liberal about things, and my mum is very kind and I think that has affected Dad's opinions, and we all stand by one another.' The closeness of the family was as important – and strong – as ever.

Oilen also recalled that time in her brother's life. 'When he told me he was gay, my first reaction was to worry for his future,' she said. 'I didn't want him to be subjected to prejudices as a result of being a gay man. At the same time I wanted him to be able to live his life freely, which is why I wanted him to be open with Mum and Dad. He was miserable when he first left home, and I was there for him as much as I could be. I just knew by the tone of his voice on the phone when he needed us, and I'd say to Mum, "I think we should go and see Babe this weekend." He started to lose the weight around the same time. It was all to do with trying to find out who he was, and I think he feels just much more himself as a slim man. It was quite a long transitional phase and from it the butterfly emerged, and he's happy.'

This was a huge turning point in Gok's life. He had left home, he was losing half his body weight, he had come out to his family (and thus the world at large) and he was putting behind him all the more difficult experiences of the past. And at this stage, he had everything to play for. Drama school might not have worked out for him, but he was still very young, with all the opportunities the metropolis afforded him and he was casting about to see what he would be able to do. The world was his for the taking.

His professional life, however, was initially slow to take off. Gok was very short of money. He worked behind a bar and made Christmas cards and lampshades, with wire he found at the bottom of his garden in Kilburn, north London, while he was learning how to do hair and make-up. It was dispiriting at times, and there were moments when he needed those visits from his family. But time passed and he continued to learn his trade.

But life certainly wasn't easy. Gok also worked in pubs and clubs to make a living, to say nothing of stints in call centres. 'Oh yeah, I've worked in a million call centres,' said Gok. 'And, do you know what? I was pretty bloody good at it.' It was a defiant attitude in latter years, but at the time was a source of intense frustration. Waiting for a career to take off can be hard going.

Gradually, however, work began to materialise. Gok was getting to know this new world, getting to know London and planning for the future. He was also exposed to the kind of shops he had never seen before. 'I remember walking down Bond Street when I first moved to London, aged 20, and thinking, "One day…" because we never had anything like that when we were younger,' he recalled.

Indeed, Gok was going from being relatively unsophisticated to someone who knew his way about town. Indeed, this was as much a part of the learning process as anything else. He was now exposed to high fashion of the haute couture kind rather than the high street, as well as sophisticated restaurants and bars – the world in which his clients moved and in which he was to move himself. It was a crucial stage to go through, still in relative anonymity, but preparing himself for the big time all the while.

As he persevered, so his client list began to build up. Big names began to come to the fore. Gok styled, amongst others, Bryan Ferry, All Saints, Damien Lewis, Erasure, Vanessa Mae, Wade Robson, Lauren Laverne, Wet Wet Wet and Johnny Vaughan. One commission led to another: people began to pass on his details. The industry began to take note of this tall, gentle Anglo-Chinese stylist they found in their midst.

As his name and reputation grew, so magazines began to be interested in his work. *Tatler* used him, as did *Glamour*. He also styled for *Times Style*, *Marie Claire*, *Cosmopolitan*, *The Face*, *Afisha Mir*, *Clash* and *People*. He was working with famous photographers, too: Rankin, Mike Owen, Tony McGee, Arthur Elgort and Jason Joyce. He was getting the all-important credits for his work now, and coming to the notice of people who were going to be of considerable use to him. There was a change in the air, and Gok was doing increasingly well.

Gok himself felt the change. Asked in 1997 when he knew he'd become successful, he replied, 'When I turned down a job because I didn't want to do it. That's when I knew I'd made it because I could afford to turn the work down. I was very pleased to get in *Glamour* magazine. It's very glossy. I did All Saints for them last year and it was nice to work with them.'

Finally, he began to make his way. Initially Gok worked for mainly for magazines, but made the move across into television, which is where he was finally to make his name. His early work was for *MTV Shakedown*, *GMTV*, *LK Today*, *Battle of the Sexes*, *The Wright Stuff*, *Make Me a Grown Up*, *The*

*Xtra Factor* and *T4*. He proved enormously popular with the people he worked with, as he continues to do now, while his hard work and professionalism made him an asset to have around. For all his flamboyance, Gok was not a prima donna and his work always came up to exacting standards. Increasingly he was well spoken of, and television executives began to wonder if they might just have another star on their hands. There was certainly no one else like Gok on television: could he possibly have what it takes?

The most important of the jobs that came his way during this period was *Big Brother's Little Brother*, for this was the time that Channel 4 executives began to think that their larger than life, Anglo-Chinese stylist, just brimming over with personality, might actually be up to fronting a television series all by himself. 'Channel 4 had seen me doing bits and bobs and asked me to do a screen test,' said Gok. 'Within a week I'd signed a contract and we were going for it. I've been doing fashion for years so I'm not afraid of being on camera but I never went into this wanting to be a celebrity.'

That series was to be *How to Look Good Naked*. After the best part of a decade waiting for his big break, Gok Wan was on his way.

# 4
# HOW TO LOOK GOOD NAKED

It was 27 June, 2006, and Gok was wild with excitement. His very own show, *How to Look Good Naked* was due to go out that night. The programme was the first of eight: if it went well, it would turn Gok into a star. If no one watched, or everyone hated it, then he had a perfectly respectable job as a stylist to go back to, but fame and fortune wouldn't be his. Which way was it going to go? For Gok, the stakes could hardly have been higher. He had, after all, aspired to be on the small screen in a different capacity when he went to drama school: now he was going to end up in people's sitting rooms after all.

The press, meanwhile, was intrigued by this unlikely new talent on the screen. The tales about Gok's past weight problems had become public, while his approach was utterly different from brusque style queens Trinny and Susannah.

Everything he said was from a sympathetic point of view: 'I've never met a woman who didn't have body image problems,' he said before the show went out. 'Even celebrities worry about how they look. The women on the show have a hate-hate relationship with their bodies, to the point where they can't undress in front of their partners.' It was very different from what the viewing public had been used to: no barking and no criticism.

Again, a great deal of what he said was just plain common sense, which, mixed with his evident enthusiasm, was eminently appealing. 'Standing badly can make you look as if you've gained 10lbs,' said Gok. 'I can slim you down by changing your clothes. I love my job. I cry with joy almost every single day, seeing these women coming into their own. This show is about admitting who you are and celebrating it.' This was exactly what Gok had done himself. He had also recreated himself to a certain extent, and found confidence after doing so: that was exactly what he was giving to the women who came on the show.

The show started as it meant to go on. The first edition featured 46-year-old Susan Sharpe, a size 14-16, who announced, 'I'd call myself fat, ugly and awful,' and who hadn't let even her husband see her naked in three years. She ended the show proudly strutting about in just bra and knickers, beaming at the camera. Gok had transformed her view of herself, the first of the countless occasions on which he was to do so.

There was some curiosity from the media as to what the

show would be like. *HTLGN* featured in several newspapers' 'Pick of the Day' columns: the next day the reviewers were unsure what to make of it all. There was quite a lot of talk about Gok's glasses, but most seemed to think this was just another television makeover show with a twist – the display in undies at the end, with the women in question happy to allow their naked or nearly naked bodies to be pictured magnified many times on the wall of a tall building. There was some acknowledgement that Gok was suggesting ways in which women could make themselves look better without surgery, but some critics got it quite badly wrong, complaining that they found Gok irritating and coming up with such phrases as, 'Gok not to wear' and, 'A load of Gok and bull'.

But if Gok found the criticism demoralising, he didn't show it. After all, the people that mattered, the public, were warming to him massively. The women who appeared on his show clearly adored him, and he was beginning to find he was being recognised – and embraced – on the street, too. It was the start of a sharp and unexpected ascent to fame, which he handled very well. The adulation that was to start heading in his direction did not go to his head; the tightness and the security of his family background meant he kept his feet on the ground.

Viewers and previewers were not put off by the barbed remarks of the critics. The following week, Gok still featured in many of the 'Pick of the Day' lists, and this time the show featured Claire Green. Claire, a mother of two, loathed her stomach and saw in her svelte sister everything she once was; Gok came to the rescue and restored her self esteem. Then there was Roberta Fox Braddock, a steelworker from South Wales, who dressed in masculine clothes to hide herself and who hated her body so much she wouldn't undress in front of her husband of 20 years. Specifically she felt she had a huge bum: Gok helped to calm those fears, too.

The next one up was Zoe Cobdon, a 27-year old Londoner who loathed her size 12 body, hardly obese but a source of torment to her. Commentators pointed out that she was a pretty woman with curves, but this highlighted exactly the service Gok was providing: these women were not seeing themselves as they really were, and he was helping them to come to terms with their bodies, whatever the shape. Writing about this episode, one reviewer called it, 'This refreshing show,' pointing out that what Gok was doing was to try to make women feel happy about themselves.

He was succeeding, too. The programme continued to pull in respectable viewing figures, and rather more positive comments as the difference in Gok's approach from Trinny and Susannah became increasingly clear. The show was, as Gok had explained, about celebrating women as they are, rather than telling them they looked rubbish and needed surgery before they walked out of the house in the evening. Interest in this radical approach continued to grow. Then came the case of Emma Wright.

Emma Wright, 37, took part in the first series, but hers was a more controversial appearance than any so far. She was a teacher in the junior section of Streatham and Clapham High School in south London, an independent school that charged £7,632 a year. Her pupils, aged eight, were delighted to find that their teacher was about to strip off on television, with pictures projected 100ft tall on the wall of Waterloo Station – so much so, they texted each other to find out exactly when she would be on. The Girls' Day School Trust, which owned the school, was bemused. Emma herself, meanwhile, was adamant that she hadn't realised what was going on.

'There was nothing in the ad about being naked, that was way down the line,' she said. 'It was only when I saw the contract and the name of the show that I balked at it, but the programme-makers said they just needed an eye-catching title. They kept me in the dark. I turned up each day not knowing what I was doing. On the day of the photoshoot they literally sat me down and asked if I was prepared to go naked. I agreed but said what I would and wouldn't allow to be shown including my rude bits, my teeth and my sticky-out ears. When I took my robe off I did cry. It was such a momentous step.'

The idea of a teacher allowing herself to be shown naked on television resulted in a degree of uproar. The story was taken up in the press and involved parties, including teachers and parents were all called upon to comment on the fuss. Gok himself had a measured response to the furore. 'The women who come on the show genuinely want some help to change their lives,' he said. 'We want the whole thing to be spontaneous so we did not tell them what they would be doing until the actual show.'

The Girls' Day School Trust, which owned the school, adopted an understanding view. 'We are of course interested in anything that may affect one of our schools and its standing in the community,' said a spokeswoman. 'We will discuss the programme with the school once people are back from their summer break. Miss Wright has taken part in this programme in a personal capacity. It is a series made by a reputable production company for a national broadcaster to be shown before the 9pm watershed. As it is shown before 9pm I do not imagine it would make uncomfortable viewing for young people. I understand that the programme was around the all-important issue of women's self-confidence and learning to value themselves and these are issues which we would support wholeheartedly.'

Parents at the school took differing views. 'We knew she was doing the programme,' said Marzena Scanlan, who had an eight-year-old daughter in Emma's class. 'She had bad dress sense and wore very unflattering stuff. Featuring naked on TV may not be the best thing from a career point of view but it's nothing to distract her from being a good teacher.'

Christine Di Ahna, whose daughter was also in the class, disagreed. 'She took two weeks off, during which the children had to have a supply teacher,' she said. 'She should have done it in her own time.'

It caused a good deal of amusement, to say nothing of generating publicity for the show. Indeed, *HTLGN* was fast becoming cult viewing, so much so that considerable attention was being paid to the people who'd agreed to appear. And some of them really did appear to need help. Next up was Leana Grech, a 33-year-old mother who loathed her body so much she hadn't had sex in four years, and would cut the labels off clothes so she wasn't reminded of her size. Like quite a few other of the women on the show, she covered herself in shapeless clothing in order to hide herself and had a fear of shop changing rooms. Could Gok help? Yes. His sympathetic and understanding approach was by now proving itself to be far more effective than the hectoring type: the fact that he was scoring one success after another was evidence of that.

Another participant was Dorothy Pearlman, 47, a nurse with a dreadful body image, who ultimately managed to peel off almost entirely for the show. Dorothy, originally from Edinburgh and now living in Essex, was a mother of three who had gone from a size eight to a 14, and was not at all happy with the way she looked. Gok managed to change that.

'I have to admit that when Gok asked me to whip off my pants, I put the foot down,' Dorothy said afterwards, as she celebrated her success. 'My family were not comfortable with it so my pants stayed on in the end. I think if it hadn't been for my husband and my kids, I'd have been carried away because the shots were tastefully done. I'm stunned I managed to go through with the show. I was proud to see a 30ft blown-up picture of me on the side of a building in Notting Hill.'

Dorothy's case was a real eye-opener as to the problems bad body image caused: it inhibited so much that she wanted to do. 'Before the show, I couldn't even go in the swimming pool,' she said. 'I found I was obsessed with covering myself up. I'm quite confident but behind closed doors I couldn't look in the mirror because it made me physically sick. My husband Jonathan thinks I'm being ridiculous when I moan. Your sex life is a big talking point on the show but that wasn't an issue for us. Somehow I've overcome my hatred of my body when it comes to making love with my husband.'

Dorothy's husband Jonathan, a teacher, was concerned, however. 'He worried I would be exploited — that I'd be chewed up and spat out for entertainment,' she explained. 'And he was worried about what other people would think. It was hard for him during filming — I was looking after me for once. The worst bit was standing in front of three mirrors. I was distraught. But Gok is incredible and eventually I was in my underwear giggling while he was laughing. You realise how silly we are. I don't think I'll become a naturist but wearing a bathing costume is no issue now and my confidence is well and truly boosted. I was swimming with my son at the weekend. I've confronted my biggest fear — and won.'

By now the show was attracting serious attention. Newspapers began to cotton on to how popular it was, and quite how much women seemed to like Gok. *HTLGN* had crept first from the television pages to the news pages, with the help of people like Emma Wright: now the very style of the show was being duplicated with the help of Gok himself. Newspapers were asking their readers if they'd like makeovers, while Gok dispensed excellent advice: 'Let the mirror be your best friend,' he counselled. 'Wear good underwear. Dress for your body. Avoid sunbeds. Look after your skin.' It all made sense and women lapped it up. Gok was becoming the most talked-about stylist around.

It was at this point that Trinny and Susannah left *What Not to Wear*, prompting an industry look at television makeover shows: *HTLGN* was called a 'modest little gem' by one commentator. For the first time, doubts about Trinny and Susannah's long-term future surfaced: was it possible that one day Gok would overtake them in the field they had made their own? And while Gok had already become accustomed to styling the stars, now even more were coming to him. All Saints had seen the programme and wanted Gok to style them for their video *Rock Steady*. Gok got them into PVC: 'The girls watched Gok's programme and loved how he made everyday women feel good about themselves,' said a source close to All Saints.

It wasn't just All Saints who were being influenced by the new television sensation. Everyone else now seemed to want to be photographed with their kit off as well. Although he might not have realised it at the time, Gok was beginning to influence nationwide trends. One national group of photographic studios, Venture New Generation, reported that increasing numbers of women were asking for tasteful nude shots of themselves, something that was being put down to the 'Gok effect'. It was no longer a case just of how to look good naked, but to be naked in a portrait shot.

'There's been a 50 per cent increase in naked photography since the programme,' said Anton Artenenkov, a photographer for Venture. 'Before, nude photography was generally limited to hazy "boudoir" style images, which were perhaps a little seedy. Our style is modern, tasteful and arty. We have couples, mothers with babies, women in their forties and fifties and even hen parties posing nude. Recently, a stag party of 20 men posed for a *Full Monty* style picture at our studio in Ormskirk, Lancashire.'

Howard Lipman, director of photography at the company, agreed. 'Women, especially, are getting much more confident about revealing their real selves and bodies on camera and are looking to create a beautiful, natural image,' he said. 'Reasons can include capturing themselves at the most womanly stage of their lives – during pregnancy – or as they reach a birthday milestone when they want to look back and reflect. Reality-style shows have given women the confidence to do this, be proud of their bodies and the resulting imagery is a celebration of who they are.'

By the end of the first series, the producers knew they had a success on their hands. Gok himself was being widely talked about and for such a newcomer to the screen had become well known very quickly. The show continued to attract some dismissive reviews right until the end, but what became apparent was that they were all by men. Male television reviewers just could not see the point of Gok, nor understand why women loved him so much.

Women, on the other hand, got the idea of the show and they absolutely adored Gok. And it must be said, his was a novel approach. It was not just Trinny and Susannah who had made women feel bad about themselves: a whole industry, not least in the shape of women's magazines, was doing likewise. Everywhere women were being bombarded with advice about how to make themselves thinner, less wrinkled, younger looking, less cellulite ridden and generally less hideous; meanwhile newspapers and magazines were only too happy to feature any celebrity who was not quite looking their best. Women were being encouraged in their self-loathing and, more to the point, encouraged to spend a great deal of money to do something about it. There were many vested interests in making woman feel bad.

Given all of this, it was virtually unprecedented for someone to come along and tell women they were fine the way they were, especially someone as appealing as Gok. Gill Hudson in *The Independent* certainly scented the wind of change: 'He was actually rather nice to the people who appeared on his programme and, in the process, generated the distinct sound of a genre moving on,' she wrote. 'If they're not terribly careful, T&S could find themselves looking so last season.' It was a very prescient remark.

Given all of this, it was no surprise that the show was commissioned for a second series. Meanwhile, there was increasing interest in Gok himself. He would become tired of talking about it eventually, but the tale of his huge weight loss continued to exert fascination to everyone who heard about it, and Gok himself realised it added a certain something to his intrigue. 'I was really fat,' he told one interviewer. 'Even when I was humungous, I'd still rock up in a nice waistcoat and feel fabulous about myself. It was only in my late teens that I began slimming down. I enjoy being a nice person.'

He did indeed, and the public loved him in return. Gok's open admissions about his own weight problems, meanwhile, endeared him to a wider audience. Here was a man who was not only unafraid to admit he'd once been grossly overweight, but who was prepared to show his vulnerable side on television. Trinny and Susannah had both had past woes themselves, if it came to that, but these days both seemed to emit a steely air invincibility. There was no way that could be said of Gok.

In early 2007, *How to Look Good Naked* began its second run. Gok was now becoming an established industry figure: when *The Sun* began a campaign about the use of size-zero girls as models, he was happy to lend his voice. 'There are thin girls but to be naturally a size zero, you'd have to be three feet tall to be healthy,' he said. 'For a woman of five foot nine inches to be that size is unnatural.' He was right, and because women loved him and liked his sympathetic approach, they listened to him. He was beginning to use his celebrity to do some real good.

Gok was also beginning to expand his remit from the

original format of the show. The team behind *HTLGN* took their 'Bod Pod' to Ocean Terminal shopping centre in Edinburgh one weekend in order to find women who would strip off and talk about their relationship with their bodies. They were to make short video clips out of these interviews in order to use them on the show: about 20 women went on to take part. The programme clearly had touched a raw nerve that said something about the state of the nation, or at least the negative thinking of its womenfolk. It was exactly in tune with what women across the country were thinking. It had its finger on the feminine pulse.

*HTLGN* was becoming water-cooler television: the type of show you gathered around the water cooler in the office to discuss the next day. As the new series began, there was no shortage of women willing to take part. First up was Liz Marlow, a former blonde bombshell who'd come to hate her body after having children (a common complaint on the show). Liz, again like other participants, dressed to conceal in loose-fitting fleeces rather than show her all. By the time Gok had finished with her, she was wearing a corset and sashaying down the catwalk at a lingerie show.

Next on the programme was Helen Thompson, who hid her figure under size-20 clothes: she too succumbed to the Gok brand of charm. By now Gok was becoming known for cheeky jokes — he had a particular penchant for women's breasts — and occasional shock tactics, all of which endeared him to the nation even more. He was certainly lapping up every minute of it.

'I call myself a doctor, I sort out people's problems,' he said. 'Everyone should feel the absolutely magical world of image control through clothing – it's such a tool for life. Isn't it wonderful to be able to walk into a room and tell 30 strangers who you are without saying a single word?' Gok had been able to do that for some time – first in his large stage, and now in his sleek one. He was attracting a great deal of comment because of his own stylish appearance and personality, which all added to the allure.

Gok put the show's success down to one thing: he actually liked women. 'I've always been influenced by my sister Oilen – a wonderfully intelligent woman who is Dawn French kind of sexy,' he said. 'A lot of gay male designers don't like women, but that's so not me: I'm a woman lover. Although I prefer to sleep with men, I think women are much sexier than guys and I don't understand the obsession some fashion people have with making them look like young boys.' That, in a nutshell, was Gok's appeal: he liked women, didn't want them to look like men and wanted them to celebrate their curves. It's no surprise the nation fell for his charm.

Gok was as relieved as anyone that the show was doing so well. 'I was in fear at first that it would be something for guys to ogle, but the sexual side of it is masked by the empowerment of the female body,' he said. 'It's the first show in the world that says, "Don't change, don't exercise." I respect Trinny and Susannah, but they've made a career out of being intimidating, whereas I actually enjoy being a nice person.'

He'd put his finger on it right there. No one could quite believe that this stylish man with such a starry clientele could actually take normal, sometimes slightly portly women, and actually make them feel happy about they way they looked. Trinny and Susannah's glory days were drawing to an end: the nation had tired of their bossiness and wanted a gentler alternative. And that was Gok.

As people continued to be fascinated by Gok, he continued to reveal more about himself. Children? Why not? 'I would really love to have children one day,' he remarked. 'I think I would make a very good mum-stroke-dad. My children would be very well dressed with absolutely no body issues.' That would be unlike the next participant in the show, Lisa Mayall, 36, who had such low self-esteem she hadn't had a haircut or shaved her legs for two years. Single, Lisa was looking for love, but realised that being so unkempt was not going to help her in her quest. Could Gok help? Yes, he could.

Next on was Leanne, who never left the house without thick black tights because she hated her legs so much, hadn't let her husband see her naked for five years and when they did get intimate – 'I have a special pair of tights.' Gok's answer to this was clever lingerie, that supported and controlled where it was needed most, along with the sexy stuff. 'It says, "I'm foxy, I'm a vixen, I'm risqué!"' he cried. The women loved it and so did the viewers.

Trinny and Susannah had just returned to the screen, but Gok was careful always not to be dismissive about them. And he put his own gentler style, down to his career. 'I'm a working stylist,' he said. 'I wouldn't be able to get booked with an A-list celebrity and say "Right, your tits are too big, your arse is too big." I'd never work with that artist again. Ninety-eight per cent of the time I have to be very diplomatic with the people I'm working with. Stylists are not bitches, we aren't horrible people. My job on *Naked* is to make it looks like they've had £10,000 of surgery. I have to get their confidence to a level where they can pull off the shoot at the end, where they're photographed naked, and make them feel wonderful and proud of what they've done.

'I don't compare myself to Trinny and Susannah. They're doing their thing. It might not be to my taste but that's just my opinion. I've never seen their show.' That was damning with faint praise, but otherwise, Gok remained resolutely diplomatic about the two women. It was a wise move – a war of words might have dented his own image, which remained resolutely straightforward and kind.

By now Gok had been exposed to a fair few women who were not pleased with their body shape and was in some position to judge on the state of the nation. 'Have I been surprised by the number of women who don't like the way they look?' he asked. 'No. I kind of expected it, to be honest. We're a nation of self-loathers and pick up on what we don't like before saying what we do. Women need to address the idea that bodies change. If you look in the mirror and your body isn't the same as it was when you were 20, whether you like it or not, that's the moment when you can start addressing it. If you hide it away, it doesn't mean it's not there any more. You have to form a relationship with your body again. A lot of it is about acceptance.'

Those were very wise words from someone who knew what it was like to look in the mirror and not like what he saw. But nor did he flatter when confronted with his subjects. 'I'm very honest,' he said. 'I'm not going to say "You're not pear-shaped" if you are. But I take on the women as if they're friends of mine because that's the way I know how to deal with people's problems. I spend eight weeks with them so a friendship happens slowly and naturally. They have to open up to me for it to work, and once their confidence is up I introduce new fashions and help them form a new relationship with their body.'

When put like that, it was clear why Gok was beating the opposition hands down. However successful they might have been when they started, Trinny and Susannah's approach did not do much towards creating trust, while it was clear that some of the women Gok was working him developed a great attachment to the man who was helping them to love themselves.

The work did, however, also take its toll. Gok was dealing with people who had very low self-esteem and the level of comfort and advice he was providing them with took it out of him as well. 'After filming I have to vent because I've taken on all that raw emotion from eight people,' he continued. 'If I harboured it I think I'd be completely fucked. My best friend Elaine is amazing. She takes a phone call from me every night and I'm like "right... blah, blah, blah." Then I call my mum, sister, brother, dad... I think some people think I'm this great big ball of confidence but I know how it feels not to like what you're looking at in the mirror. It sounds really boring but I have a complete love for what I do. I genuinely like the women on the show. I'm not very good at many things but this I can do. Everyone has to find their niche in life.'

Gok had found his niche and then some: stylist, certainly, but in some ways a guru for the needy and self-loathing. Watching him gave women who hated themselves hope. Certainly it was crucial he had the kind of personality that he did to make the show work, but Gok was just getting better and better at drawing people out and giving them confidence in themselves. He was becoming every woman's gay best friend.

For that was the other secret to it: had Gok been heterosexual, then women would have been very unlikely to entrust themselves to him in the way they did. He was not averse to prodding and poking them and teasing them about their bosoms, but the women all knew it was just being done in jest. Nor was there the threat of any emotional game playing: they could trust Gok just as they could trust another woman. The format of the show, the idea that they should be made to feel happy, and above all, Gok's effervescent personality, had all gone to make the new venture an astounding success.

# 5
# GOK 'N' ROLL

**B** y the end of the second series of *Naked* – as everyone was beginning to refer to it – it was clear that Gok had become a star. It was no longer just women who adored him: the nation was taking him to its heart. Jonathan Ross summed up the prevailing mood when he told Gok he was a 'lovely man'. His gentleness, his openness about his own past problems and his determination that women should be encouraged to make the most of themselves and not be hectored for being too big, all endeared him to the wider public.

There comes a moment when someone goes from being a new face on television to an established figure: that moment for Gok was now. He was much loved and regularly mobbed when going out in public, and he found that he was under much greater scrutiny than before. He was regularly being asked to comment on all matters fashion-related, and was writing regularly with advice. Fan mail continued to pour in by the sack load and television bosses realised they had a hot property on their hands.

Gok's appearance on *Friday Night with Jonathan Ross* illustrated just how popular he'd become. From the moment he walked on the show he was greeted with cheers from the audience, before admitting he was feeling rather nervous. 'Imagine you're like a fat bird and I'm you, calming you down,' Ross advised, a comment Gok took with remarkably good grace. The two went on to discuss the bullying Gok had endured at school – 'Big puff homo' was what Gok recalled them saying and that he, 'used humour to bat the attention away' – before venturing on to the subject of his size when young.

The audience audibly gasped when they heard he used to be 21 stone. 'That was a whole lot of chow mein,' said Gok, before adding that he'd looked like 'a six-foot Chinese ladyboy. I looked like a dyke.' This was another clue to his popularity: his propensity for self-deprecation. There were not many public figures who would be so hard on themselves.

At this point a picture of a very large Chinese child wearing spectacles tucking into a bowl of food flashed up in the background. 'That is so not me,' said an unfazed Gok, adding, 'But very similar. Good research.' He beamed with good humour. Ross pointed out that in addition to the weight, the glasses looked the same.

The conversation turned on to how *Naked* came about. 'It

was a collaboration,' said Gok. 'We wanted to do a show about fashion using the word "naked" and we wanted to strip down what stylists really do. We're not bitches. I as a stylist have to go in and work with what there is already. But I did not know it was going to be the way it was.'

Of course, the use of the word 'naked' had been a canny ploy. It had been bound to attract attention, which it did, but it also appealed to the deep-seated fear of so many women in the country: that they were never going to be able to look good naked. The title was intriguing, but also held a promise that was the dearest wish of every woman.

And that really did include just about everyone. Gok went on to say that he had never styled anyone, male or female, who had been perfectly happy with their body, and that in some ways it was actually more difficult for the famous. 'Celebrities get it worse, as they are constantly confronted with their own image,' he said. Ross quoted the statistic that three quarters of women spend time fretting over their own body every day: 'Till now, women have never had a sense of community,' replied Gok. 'Those statistics have created a sense of community and made them realise they're not on their own. What I do is to make them look better than before with what they've got.'

The interview was interspersed with shots of one of Gok's many triumphs: a woman called Lucy, who was first shown staring at her reflection in the mirror clad only in her underwear. 'Horrible. Shapeless,' she muttered, as she seemed almost to fold in on herself in despair at the way she looked. The end of the show then came up in which a transformed Lucy, with exactly the same figure, stalked triumphantly down a catwalk, before triumphantly throwing off her cloak to reveal that she was still clad in underwear, but considerably sexier underwear, and she didn't mind a hugely magnified picture of her being beamed out to the audience. The crowd roared, both on the original and during the interview.

Another factor of which the audience approved was that Gok was pleasingly modest about what he did, in direct contrast to those who appeared to believe that in some way they were above hoi polloi. 'Fashion's not rocket science,' he said. 'It's not hard. It's about being confident, being experimental, being creative. When I was researching by reading fashion books recently, I was totally confused. I just went back to the basics.' The audience lapped it up.

His approach, too, was informed greatly by his own experience. 'I have to be diplomatic, but mostly honest,' he told another interviewer. 'If someone is pear-shaped and they are saying "I hate my ass," I can't say "No, you're fine." but I can say "You have fabulous tits." I don't believe in being horrible to get results. That's bullying, I've had my fair share of that in the past.' He had indeed, and it was that past that had shaped him. For all his flamboyance, Gok still had something of the vulnerable child about him. He was not overbearing. He still gave the impression of wanting to be loved.

And he was now in demand everywhere. He signed up to do a newspaper column dispensing fashion tips, and it was reported that Peter Jones, of *Dragons' Den* fame, had hired Gok to take his girlfriend Tara shopping. (Well, it was her birthday.) He was being interviewed everywhere: various disclosures about Gok's lifestyle included the fact that he liked going to the café TPT in Chinatown for a big bowl of noodles and 'me time', and that 'there are two types of woman – those who don't do anything with accessories and those who wear so many they look like a Christmas tree.'

It was a wickedly accurate description of the British female, but non-judgemental, as ever. In fact, it was hard not to suspect that Gok rather approved of women who were a little OTT. His own appearance, with that blond streak at the front of the head against that ebony black hair, his extraordinary collection of earrings, his statement glasses and his very striking wardrobe, did not betoken a man who wished to hide away from the world. They spoke of someone who was right in there at the centre of the action.

Indeed Gok was having the time of his life. As well as the bohemian London lifestyle he'd already been enjoying, he was now a media figure, too. He retained his freshness, his youthfulness, and still managed to lead a private life without too much attention coming his way, although when he was out in public, much of what he did was reported on. He revealed his delight at being asked for ID at the age of 32 when going to a club, and that he enjoyed 'dancing around cheesy 1980s music with my friends'. His was such an innocent enjoyment of the fame and good fortune that had come his way that it was impossible not to be pleased for him.

Like so many celebrities, Gok was now being asked for his opinion on anything and everything, and he was happy to oblige. 'I would pay more attention to the health service,' he said in response to one questioner about the state of Britain today. 'I feel for the nurses – the conditions, the hours and the money is terrible. We are lucky we have the NHS but we need to keep it number one by investing enough money.' This was also a reminder that for all the fame and wealth that was now coming his way, Gok grew up in a poverty-stricken, rough council estate. He came from the real world, not a rarified version of it, and understood the women he took beneath his wing.

Gok was also now much happier in himself. Although he'd been out and accepted as such by his family for years, the fact that the public clearly adored him made him much more relaxed in his own skin. He was also far more accepting of his mixed racial heritage than he had been, and the fact that he was happy to talk about it conveyed a refreshingly honest approach. 'As a result of the bullying and the environment I grew up in I didn't come out to my family until my early twenties,' he told one interviewer. 'I was really scared of losing them. Being gay isn't well accepted in Chinese culture. I used to insist that I was English, but I'm proud of my Chinese heritage now and I've found out a lot about it. Anyone who's gay has to struggle. I grew up in Leicester in this huge council estate. For an incredibly camp mixed-race kid, it was a dangerous and hurtful place.'

Now there were advantages to being gay, especially in

Gok's line of work. He became very close to the women he worked with, and his sexuality made that easier. So did being male. 'Styling someone is incredibly personal, it's not just manhandling their body into a dress,' he said. 'You have to get into their mind. You have to be trusted. Definitely [it helps that I'm gay]. There's no intrusion sexually and, because I'm a man, there's no competition.'

That was also something that set him apart from other television stylists. Apart from Trinny and Susannah, telly's other most prominent member of the breed was Nicky Hambleton-Jones. In both those cases there was always a slight feeling that here was one woman criticising another, and of course, in Gok's case, that simply didn't exist. The dynamic was totally different: the shows charted the trusting relationship between a man and a woman, even if there would never be a sexual element to it. It all made for a very different kind of show.

The first series of *Naked* was now going out on cable, a sure sign that Gok was becoming television gold. Gok, meanwhile, was revealing more details of his personal style. His appearance – so tall and so personally stylish – continued to fascinate: the public was becoming increasingly curious about his own look. And it was a distinctive one. The sharp glasses and the exaggerated earrings made him instantly recognisable, while a slight outrageousness hinted of an irrepressible personality, which indeed was what came out on screen.

But Gok was adamant that away from the spotlight, he

wasn't that full-on. 'I'm more spit and sawdust than people think,' he said. 'I groom myself for work, but when you spend your life making things pretty, you can't be bothered at home. I'm straight into my tracksuit. I love tracksuits, maybe not in a velour-Ugg-boots-hair extensions way, but my bag usually contains my black Stussy tracksuit.' It was certainly not a look he wore out in public: as far as everyone else was concerned, his appearance was always immaculate. No one had ever seen him let the side down.

Gok was also a gym bunny. He had been for years now, ever since that huge weight loss, but now that he was appearing regularly on television, his appearance was more important. He worked hard at it, too, although pleasingly, his concern was no longer about how to lose weight but how to keep it on. 'A lot of weights and not too much cardio,' he said to one interviewer who asked him how he worked out at the gym. 'I'd lose too much weight otherwise. I'm a bit greedy, though. I look around and see people doing fun stuff and I'm saying to my trainer: "What's she doing? She's punching something. I want to do that…" When I'm there I get an immense rush of endorphins, but I crash as soon as I get home.'

Gok was, in fact, frequently critical of his lifestyle, confessing that while he might be keeping the weight down, his habits were still very bad. He was, he confessed, a big drinker and heavy smoker, but the fact was that now he had attained the appearance he wanted, he was prepared to work hard to keep it that way. And any unhealthiness in his lifestyle was offset by the sheer amount of energy he expounded in tearing about the country, not least because Gok was determined, now that he had achieved such success, to make the most of it. His parents had always worked hard and now that all these opportunities had come his way, Gok was determined to do so, too.

He could also be very critical of his own appearance, showing himself to be quite as body dysmorphic as any of the women he helped. 'I'd change my nose first,' he said. 'I've got a satsuma for a nose. And I hate that when I laugh I've got a big double chin. My jaw squashes it all out at the sides. And I really hate my feet. I've got one scabby, dry foot and one pretty foot.' Of course, just as with the women he styled, no one else would have noticed these perceived faults, but to Gok, whose life was in making people think about their appearance, they were loud and clear.

More and more it was obvious that Gok's often professed sympathy for women who had a difficult relationship with their bodies really was in keeping with his feelings about his own. Gok was now a handsome man, becoming more so as he grew older. Self-acceptance meant he had grown into his own skin and it suited him. But, of course, he worked in the fashion industry, not a place where many are secure of their looks, and Gok was as prone to self-doubt as anyone. The little bullied boy was still not so far away.

But Gok had moved on, and nowhere was this more obvious than through his relationship with food. 'I've changed a hell of a lot,' said Gok. 'I don't seek happiness through food, unless I'm going to a really nice restaurant. I'm conscious of what I eat, but it doesn't rule my life.' It had been an addiction and he'd overcome it. The new Gok had emerged stronger than before.

Gok mania continued. The Spice Girls were currently in the news and everyone wanted his view on them. 'I hear they're getting a dream team together to style them,' he said. 'I'd love to show them how to work it without their clothes on.' His comments, as they tended to by now, made the news. He was roped in as a judge for Specsavers' Spectacle Wearer of the Year competition: a Scottish student called Sara Pender, 18, was the winner and Gok's presence generated a huge amount of publicity.

Indeed, Gok was on something of a roll with the Scots. *Naked* was returning for a third series in November 2007, and to mark it, Gok was to take part in a live version on stage in Glasgow, *How To Look Good Naked – Live*. The two-hour show was to take place at the Armadillo auditorium, and the producers were to be The Comedy Unit. There was some smiling at this: they were also the team behind Rab C Nesbitt, not known for his natty attire.

'He's so keen to do it, even though nothing like this has been tried before,' said an insider on the show. 'Gok's a natural for the stage. He deals with women struggling with an extreme lack of body confidence and does all he can to help rebuild it without having to resort to nip and tuck. He has no fear of tackling a live audience.' Even so, it was a brave move – live audiences in Glasgow were not for the faint-hearted. And given that no one had ever tried anything like this before, Gok was charting new territory. Would he be able to pull it off?

In the run-up to the next series of *Naked* and the live show, Gok himself continued to be a vociferous champion of the way women really are, pointing out that expectations for today's women are totally out of kilter. 'The UK perception of beauty is totally out of whack,' he told one interviewer. 'We're incredibly confused about what we think is attractive: women who are a size 10, but who hate their bodies; women who admire someone who is a 14, but who don't want to be a 14 themselves. We haven't a clue! We're told certain things, and we believe them. You're probably wearing that dress because you think someone else will like it. Yes, I can [make anyone look good naked]. There's no trickery involved. It's about changing attitudes. It's a very moving journey. We get through a lot of Kleenex.'

Gok also confided other, more surprising aspects of the show. For whatever reason, women felt the ability to confide in him almost immediately upon meeting, and so it was that he knew a lot of people who appeared on *Naked* no longer had sex with their partners. Once their confidence was restored, their sex life started up again. This was clearly more than just a make-over show: it was restoring something very vital to these women's psyche, and repairing their relationships with their partners. In fact, Gok was improving someone's appearance as a way of healing something more fundamental.

Gok realised how important it was, too. 'To be able to

share your body again is a massive way of judging where you are with it,' he said. 'Or having sex in more than one position, or with the light on. How liberating! We're not romantic enough about sex in this country; it's just in and out, and, "Did-you-put-the-shepherd's-pie-in-the-oven?"' It might have been a blunt way of putting it, but he was right.

Unsurprisingly, there was now a good deal of interest in Gok's own private life. He had been totally open about the fact that he was gay, but what about a partner? Was there a man in Gok's life? Well, there had been until recently, and Gok was happy to talk about that, too, although he didn't actually name names out of respect for the other person involved. 'Newly single after seven years; we split up six months ago,' he told an interviewer who enquired after his status. 'I love him to pieces. He's an amazing man, but he's not out to his family and that was a massive problem because he was going to have to be seen with me, and now people know who I am. He was also a Muslim. So I'm looking! I'm not good on my own. I crave it [a relationship] because I'm very lonely.' Lonely, but popular. Every woman in the country wanted Gok as her gay best friend.

Gok was discovering, too, that being famous could have a downside if you were looking for love. 'My friends are all getting married,' he continued. 'Being single and 33 is no longer an issue. However, being 33 and famous and single is an issue. Meeting new people is difficult. You have to go on a really hard edit to find out who really fancies you, and who just wants to sleep with you because you're famous.'

Indeed, such had been the speed with which he had become famous, that Gok was having to learn very quickly as he went along. 'There isn't such a thing as celebrity school,' he said. 'When the show first came out I didn't leave the house for seven days; I had a real breakdown about being exposed. But if people want to be mean to me there's nothing I can do to stop them. I live in fear of the gossip mags. I don't want people around me to be hurt. Because I've been quite naughty in my past! So far, though, no one seems to be that interested in me – not even the people I've been sleeping with, unfortunately.'

In actual fact, remarkably few people were mean to Gok. Male reviewers still made barbed remarks, but the truth was that he was very possibly the most popular man on television. Women adored him more than ever, and there were very few people who would dispute the fact that he was a genuinely nice man. But of course, that bullied boy was still lurking in there somewhere, which made Gok more cautious about how people perceived him than he might otherwise have been.

And he certainly knew his stuff where the fashion industry was concerned. It wasn't just that he knew the tricks of making an outfit look good: he was even up to scratch on what body shapes were more likely to end up in relationships. There were facts and figures at work here, as well as a sense of style.

He tended to share this knowledge in his own inimitable way. When told that men had it easier than women, he disagreed emphatically. 'Women have magic underwear!' he said. 'There's no such thing as tummy-tuck pants for guys. You can't readily get a pair of pants that make your cock look bigger either.' As for women's shapes – 'Women who are pear-shaped are statistically more likely to have children, and women who carry weight around their tummies are more likely to be in a relationship. Guys like women with a bit of flesh!'

This was indeed the kind of remark that Britain's army of less-than-perfect women wanted to hear. It was all very well being told that they were beautiful whatever their shape, but to hear that the plump and pear shaped really did end up happier in the relationship stakes (or, at least, were more likely to be in a relationship) was exactly the sort of encouragement they wanted to hear.

And what advice would he give women generally? 'I'm not going to pigeonhole the women of the UK,' he said. 'That is their biggest problem. But I would say: be honest with yourselves. If there's a dent in your car, you'll walk round the other way so you don't have to see it. But whatever you hate about your body is not going to go away unless you have surgery. So live with it! Celebrate it! Stop being so stupid! That's what I'd say to the women of the UK.'

And so to Glasgow, where Gok proved himself more than up to the task of charming the local beauties, with massive interest centred on the live show. By now there was much jollity about how easy he, a gay man, found it to get women to undress. His homosexuality was part of the secret, of course, but he was able to joke about himself with ease. 'It's honestly not difficult for me to get women to strip off,' he told a Scottish journalist. 'I can probably strip most women. It's amazing: straight men would want me to bottle it. I just have to look at a woman and her bits are hanging out.'

As a sort of rehearsal for the live show, Gok was styling two girls who had won a competition through the New Look fashion chain. He was clearly enjoying every second of it. 'I love a makeover,' he said. 'We're running it like the show so I knew nothing about the girls beforehand. So we have a chat then make them look fabulous – as always. What I choose depends entirely on their age, what they do for a living, their body shape, what kind of female celebrities they like, the music they like, the food they eat... everything. All of it contributes to their outfit.'

It also made them feel cosseted, looked-after and secure. That was another of Gok's secrets of success with women: he actually listened to them, took on board their views and seemed interested in what they had to say. He didn't dictate: he suggested, and what he suggested had the interests of his new friends at heart. It also made the experience far more individual. Although Gok could mete out advice for those with differing body shapes with the best of them, the fact that he bothered to find something out about his subjects made a huge difference. The women felt he really did want what was best for them.

And he did. Gok was now constantly under surveillance so there was no way he could have been putting on an act. What you saw was genuinely what you got: there were no barbed remarks slipping out when they weren't expected, no criticisms or insults and certainly no suggestion that you had previously had good taste. You merely got the undivided attention of a man who loved women in a pure way and wanted them to be happy. There was no way Gok could have bottled what he had and given it to a straight man, because there was no way a straight man would be able to think and act like Gok.

Nor was he displaying any concern about the live show at the end of the month. 'We'll have the boobs out and be doing the underwear and the "skinny in seconds" — loads of really nice stuff,' he said. 'I don't think getting them to strip will be more difficult on stage ... but then I do love a challenge. We don't tell women to lose weight and that's what makes our show so successful. A makeover isn't about telling someone they have to be completely different — it's about making over what's there already, using it as a foundation. On *Naked* we are challenging people's perceptions of beauty. Hopefully that will filter through to the rest of the world.'

By coincidence, Glasgow was also playing host to two other stylists that week — Trinny and Susannah, who were on tour to sign their latest book. Gok was his usual diplomatic self when the subject came up. 'They're doing their own job — it might not be how I would do my job, they might not be styling how I view stylists, but they are making a living. Can you imagine me, Trinny and Susannah in the same room? Bloody hell, that would be fun, wouldn't it?' This was as close as Gok ever came to direct criticism, but he clearly felt strongly about the point. Given his own soaring popularity, he was also right.

And, playing to the audience as ever, Gok then turned his attention to one very famous Scot. 'I definitely want to give Gordon Brown a makeover, he dresses hideously,' he said. 'But he's a bloke in politics, what's he to do? If the PM turned up in a fleur-de-lis Alexander McQueen jacket, MPs would shit themselves. Mind you, if he wore a fleur-de-lis jacket, I'd probably want to sleep with him.' As ever, Gok's cheekiness was part of his charm.

Newly single, Gok was determined to live life to the full. Whether he was seeking a partner or something perhaps a little more peripheral was hard to say, but he was certainly full of praise for the local men. 'I love it up here and I love Scottish boys,' he confided. 'I'm on the hunt for a new man. I'm looking for a beautiful, cute, handsome, kilt-wearing, whisky-drinking, naughty boy – I love my job but I love men more. I'm a particular lover of tartan. I hear it's true what they say about men in kilts so I can't wait to go to my first Scottish wedding. I'll be lying on the floor most of the time.'

It was a mark of Gok's charm that he could get away with that. Glaswegians are not the easiest of audiences, but then Gok was unique. It couldn't have hurt that although he was English by birth, he was half-Chinese by heritage, and so, perhaps, he was granted a little more leeway than an Englishman would have been under similar circumstances. But whatever the reason, the Glaswegians took him comprehensively to their Scottish hearts. But this was merely the beginning of the next phase. Gok and *Naked* were getting bigger and bigger, becoming ever more of a phenomenon and ever more influential to the women of Britain. There had never been anyone in the public eye quite like Gok.

# 6

# GOK WAN: PUBLIC SERVICE PROVIDER

**A**s the third series of *Naked* began to screen in November 2007, Gok's role as a stylist who also happens to change people's lives was becoming increasingly clear. Marriages were being repaired in the wake of the Gok treatment. Whole swathes of women were beginning to recover their self-esteem. He was creating a whole new fashion in television presenting, in which women were not simply poked, prodded and criticised, but made to feel they were worth something.

The new series of *Naked* attracted even more attention than its predecessors, for the simple reason that it had now a track record and the viewing public knew what an impact it was making. In some ways that presented a new challenge to Gok, for whereas formerly he was brand new to the box and had nothing to prove, now he had to show that he could maintain the momentum. But he did.

Gok's first subject was Sonya Pettigrew, a woman so unhappy about her size and large breasts that her husband hadn't seen her naked in over a year, the couple were sleeping in separate bedrooms and had even contemplated the possibility of a divorce. She had dreamed of becoming a ballet dancer, but her large breasts had put an end to that: now she taught ballet without ever looking in the mirror, no mean feat given that most ballet studios are practically lined with them.

Gok offered his usual gentle words of reassurance. 'People don't see themselves as others do,' he said. 'We need to love our bodies.' Meanwhile, other people were picking up on the way that Gok really was changing people's lives: 'Who says this show is not a public service?' asked one reviewer.

It wasn't just the show: it was Gok himself. He managed to show compassion not just for women who hated themselves, but women who really had been touched by tragedy as well. He and *Naked* joined forces with Empire Stores to give two women who really had been having a bad time of it a makeover, and the two were full of praise for what he did. Lesley Coburn, 41, a former catwalk model, lived in Widnes, Cheshire, and had been diagnosed with multiple sclerosis four years previously. Her mother had also died before the diagnosis, something Lesley hadn't really come to terms with, and her weight was yo-yoing because of the steroids she had to take to combat her illness. If anyone deserved a break, it was her and the whole experience was a huge success.

'When they showed me the final result of the makeover in the mirror I didn't believe it was me,' she said. 'I was so shocked at the change. As a result of meeting Gok I have made changes to my wardrobe. Although I still wear jeans because it's too cold for skirts, I'm wearing much nicer tops. I didn't wear them before because I'm self-conscious about the way I walk. The MS has made me limp a bit and I always felt that covering up my legs disguised the limp.'

Gok didn't just persuade her to be more adventurous in her choice of dress: he also made her feel actively considerably better about her own appearance, surely an invaluable service to someone who has MS. 'Gok said I should wear skirts to show off my legs more because they're in good shape,' said Lesley. 'He told me off for keeping them hidden.' Her happiness was undeniable, as was Gok's kindness and sympathy. Here was a woman who really had suffered tragedy and Gok had managed to help.

Indeed, he totally changed the way Lesley felt about herself. 'More importantly, he's made me realise how I can make the most of my looks,' she continued. 'It has boosted my confidence and made me feel so much happier. The two days it took were the best of my life and I loved every second.' Coming from a former model, and thus someone who might have been expected to know all about fashion already, this was high praise indeed. But then Lesley had lost all her confidence, as so many of Gok's subjects had done before her, and needed help to break out of this negative cycle of self-neglect.

The other winner of the competition was Valerie Suave, 56, a care-home worker from Northallerton, Yorkshire. She had two grown-up children and had been widowed the previous year when her husband John, who had coped for years with diabetes, had finally suffered a couple of strokes. Valerie had clearly not recovered from it: years of her husband's illness, followed by the bereavement, had taken its toll. Understandably, she had been suffering from depression and when she met Gok, she was feeling very low. But she, too, was greatly cheered by the session.

'When I first met Gok I was amazed how well he knew which clothes would suit me and at how good his ideas were,' she said. 'Because of my work I need to dress practically. Gok gave me lots of good tips on how to dress to suit my body shape.' And he did it nicely, with a great deal of sensitivity, given what Valerie had just gone through.

One of Gok's great tricks was the use of good underwear that shaped as necessary, pulled you in here and flattened you out there. Valerie was as impressed as she was amused by that. 'He showed me pants that pull you in and a push-up bra in a skin tone that won't show up under my clothes,' she said. 'I even wore this old-fashioned girdle-type thing with hooks and eyes that Gok had to do up for me. It was really funny and I had to breathe in so it would do up. He joked I'd be down to a size 10 and boy, did it make a difference to my shape.'

tepping out: Gok attending the *Women's Own* Children of Courage Awards at
Vestminster Abbey in December 2007.

*Above*: Before Gok hit the scene, Trinny Woodall and Susannah Constantine were supremely popular. Pictured here at the book launch for *What You Wear Can Change Your Life* in 2004. © PA Photos

*Below left*: Gok out and about in London with Nicole Appleton from All Saints in 2006, at the time that his career was skyrocketing. © Rex Features

*Below right*: In 2007 Gok was a guest on *The New Paul O'Grady Show*. © Rex Features

Gok poses with Twiggy Lawson and comedian David Mitchell at the British Comedy
Awards in December 2007.

*Above*: Gok onstage with Jonathan Ross and Twiggy at the British Comedy Awards.

*Below*: Gok helps to launch Tesco's Race for Life, in aid of Cancer Research UK.

Gok at the Elle Style Awards Launch at H&M, Oxford Street, London in January 2008.

*Above*: Gok surprising comedian Al Murray after appearing on his show, *Al Murray's Happy Hour*, with Dawn French in 2008.

© Rex Features

*Below*: When Tania Goodenough lost over 3 ½ stone, her husband won her a makeover from Gok in a charity auction.

© Rex Features

he name's Wan... Gok Wan: getting friendly with singer and presenter Mica Paris at The tory of James Bond – A Tribute to Ian Fleming, held at The Palladium in London, 2008.

*Above*: Hard at work, filming *How to Look Good Naked* in February 2008.   © Rex Feature

*Below left*: Gok is 'papped' on his way to the Radio 1 studios in London, 2007.   © Rex Feature

*Below right*: Such a star… Gok at the *TV Quick* and *TV Choice* Awards, September 2007.

© Rex Feature

Choosing the right underwear was, in fact, one of the most important aspects of the Gok approach. Asked about the best style advice he could give women, he replied, 'Get your foundations right. You cannot dress anything unless what's underneath is all in the right proportion.' It was a mantra he would repeat time and again.

As with Lesley, Valerie was also enormously cheered by being the centre of some fuss and attention, especially after such a difficult year. 'I felt amazing when they'd finished my makeover, so dressy and glamorous,' she said. 'It was so much fun and every time I felt nervous in front of the camera, Gok would pass me a glass of champagne and make me laugh so I'd relax. It really helped boost my confidence for the first time since I lost John. I have been renewed and can't believe that clothes could make such a difference to my confidence. The makeover and the pampering gave me such a lift.'

It is difficult to see how these two women would have benefited from attention from Trinny and Susannah, but after the Gok treatment both clearly felt revitalised. Their stories were testament to the fact that while fashion might be considered a frivolous industry in some quarters, it could and did make a significant difference to a person's well being and how they lived their lives. Disability, illness and bereavement cannot be solved by a pretty frock or good underwear, but looking and feeling better about yourself were clearly enormously beneficial.

Gok was performing a wider public service, too. His

growing army of fans were watching the show and taking advice from him about how to make a difference in their own appearance, which was in turn making a difference in their own lives. There might only have been limited numbers of women he could see when making the television show, but there was no limit to the number of women who could watch him and act in their own lives on his advice. The message to the viewers was clear: if he could make very obviously depressed women who hate themselves learn to come to terms with their body and in doing so learn to love themselves again, then you could do it, too.

And who was better placed to make women feel better about themselves than Gok? These were two unusual cases, in that the women concerned had suffered tragedy in their lives, but they certainly weren't alone in hating the way they looked. 'I always knew women felt this way, just from spending so much time styling them,' said Gok. 'It never failed to shock me when I did a job with a celebrity and even they made comments about their bodies like "I don't like this" or "I don't like that". It just confirms that all of us, regardless of our gender or fame, have issues with our bodies. We really have to change our perceptions of what's deemed attractive. There isn't such a thing as a perfect body.' This was a very different message from other make-over shows, which were based on telling people they could be perfect if only they changed everything. Gok's message? You can be gorgeous and desirable, just the way you are.

And he had been doing this long enough to know exactly

what women felt about themselves. 'The fact that their bodies have changed – from having your period to having babies and going through the menopause, women's bodies are always changing,' he said. 'Women need to get used to it, get over it and deal with what's already there because you have the ability to look fabulous and it's all about what is on the inside.'

In addition, he was so enthusiastic about every part of his work. Gok was, of course, excellent at what he did as a stylist and he was unabashed about that, too. 'I am a good judge of style because I live and breathe my industry,' he said. 'I absolutely love it. It's my hobby as well as my job. I'm self taught, I'm not trained at all so anything that happens when it comes to my style and my judgement is organic. It's not technical, it's purely a love. I think the moment you love something so much you can judge anything.'

But Gok was capable of being mischievous, too. About as openly gay as it was possible for a person to be, he couldn't resist going public about which fellow celebrities he found attractive. 'I still love Mark Owen. I'm obsessed with him,' he said. 'When I was younger, I used to deliver takeaways for my dad's fish and chip shop in my Citroen 2CV and I always played my Take That album. Mark was my ultimate heart-throb and still is. I absolutely love Ryan Phillippe and Jonathan Rhys Meyers, too, but there are also some unlikely ones. I have a bit of a crush on Simon Cowell. I've no idea why, I just think he's fit. And Gordon Ramsay – ding dong! I have such an eclectic taste in everything I do, including men. I need a different man for each outfit!'

What Gordon, Simon et al thought about Gok's homage to them is not on record, but it was certainly a sign of how times had changed. If someone like Gok had come out with a remark like that 30 years previously, their career would have been over. As it was, that comment caused a great deal of innocent enjoyment, and has been repeated endlessly ever since. Indeed, if anything Gok might have created a rod for his own back, so often has it been noted that he finds Simon Cowell attractive. But he doesn't appear to mind.

It was also pretty brave to come out with a remark like that, however, for Gok had had personal experience of where homophobia could lead. Most people took it all in good spirit, but there were still those who would find such a comment offensive and not hesitate to say so. And given how Gok had suffered in the past from people who didn't like his obvious campness, it displayed a certain boldness to do something that amounted to taking them on. It was a way of saying that the bullies had not won.

'From a very young age I knew bullying could happen and when it did, I handled it in my own way,' Gok said, on a more serious note. 'I became quite mouthy and obnoxious. We just dealt with it. Anybody that goes through any kind of social torment has to. But I come from a strong family who supported me and really were my wall of defence. We pulled through it and because of that, it's probably helped me do my job. If someone has been bullied, I want to help them even more, to prove a point to the bullies. They have no right to do that.'

But the fact was that it still happened, even now. Gok was not an inconspicuous person and there were still homophobes and racists around. 'Because of the way I look, I stick out in a crowd,' he said. 'Sometimes I have 300 people a day asking for pictures and autographs. I also get called names like "faggot" and "there's the queer from TV" or "Jackie Chan". But it's nothing more than I'd get in the playground.' In other words, having survived as a child, Gok certainly wasn't going to let abuse from adults bother him. At the same time, he was pointing out that any unpleasantness he might get today was actually on a level with the way children behave. It was a neat way to put his detractors down.

Gok risked the wrath of the homophobes in other ways, too. He was looking for marriage and children but with another man rather than a woman, and he wasn't afraid to say so. Indeed, so important was family life to him that he even contemplated stepping back from his television work if it came along. 'If I had the opportunity of getting married and having children, I might consider giving it all up,' he said. 'It was never on the cards in my last relationship. I'm an old romantic at heart and love the idea of spending the rest of my life with someone and becoming a parent – although I haven't really considered whether I'd adopt or not. I'm at the age where I'm invited to weddings and everyone's starting families, which is quite painful. I'd love all that, too.'

But with whom? And how to attain it when he seemed to spend so much time being mobbed? And there was another downside to fame. Gok's air of friendliness, to say nothing of the fact that he had visibly changed some lives, meant that shopping had become more hazardous than it had been. All it needed was for word to spread that Gok was in town, and huge crowds of women would turn up, determined to meet their idol and — who knows? — perhaps ask him for advice. There was also enormous curiosity in what Gok himself might be buying. It didn't make for an easy time.

'I constantly get asked for fashion tips, too,' said Gok. 'Going into a clothes shop is a nightmare as women follow me round to check what I'm picking out to see if I'm crap at my job. I think because I'm very down-to-earth, it automatically makes people feel comfortable coming up to me.'

Of course, this behaviour was also a testament to his success. It was the very fact that women felt so comfortable with Gok that made them love him so much, along with the fact that somehow they felt he was their friend even if they'd never actually met him. He appeared to be exposing an underbelly of pain that no one had even realised existed before: a nation of women who hated themselves and needed a sympathetic character like him to nurse them back to health. There was nothing that Gok would not turn to women's advantage: when *Naked* revealed the fact that 75 per cent of British women preferred to have sex in the dark, Gok announced, 'Next time you get turned on — don't switch off!'

Who could resist that? Gok was turning into something resembling an outrageous gay stylist crossed with the girl next door. His unfailing enthusiasm and joie de vivre, combined with genuine good nature and compassion, made him practically unique on British television. Letters were appearing in the national press praising him: he might have had his detractors and suffer the odd moment of racial or homophobic abuse, but they were a drop in the ocean compared to the number of people who loved him.

And, of course, it helped that he had been there himself. 'I'm not shy but I take my hat off to my ladies on the show,' he said. 'What they do is brilliant. When I was younger my body was my biggest enemy. I was very large and it's taken me 12 years to love the body I'm in. So I've nothing to gain from taking my kit off. I had no idea the show would be so popular and I'm still stunned by it. I don't know why women warm to me. I'm not a bitch and I'm not mean and that helps. And I've been through hard times myself. It was tough growing up as a Chinese, gay, overweight kid. I've tackled my battle with my body and now it's time to help others.'

But he freely admitted he'd never stripped in public himself – although there was an anecdote there as well. 'Not in front of people, but I've been drunk and peed in the street,' he confided. 'My nan once did it at a festival when I was younger. She got drunk on cider and weed in a bush. I'm still traumatised.'

It helped, perhaps, that he had grown up as the outsider looking in. He was neither entirely English nor entirely Chinese; his sexuality also set him apart and so, too, did his weight when young. The constant need to defend yourself and find a place in society in some way spoke out to those women who hated themselves so much. They, too, felt outside society's mainstream and that Gok, almost alone, understood. His status as an outsider made him far more observant than many other people, and this helped both in his role as a stylist and as a sympathetic ear for the distressed. His childhood might have been hard but paradoxically, it had set him up for great success.

Having led by example when he lost so much weight, Gok was qualified to talk about how to maintain a good figure, too, and his was not a culture of denial. 'Never deny yourself anything,' he said. 'Everything in moderation. So if you want it, have it. Just make sure you compromise in other areas. And to make sure you moderate the amount of water that you drink, every time you go for a wee, have a glass of water afterwards. And the more you drink the more you piss, and the more you piss the more you drink!'

Gok just couldn't contain that mischievous streak, and never was it more in evidence than when attending a celebrity-strewn event. When he attended the Scottish BAFTAs, Lorraine Kelly and James McAvoy came in for some good-natured teasing. 'I really want to see Lorraine Kelly's bangers,' said Gok, who was becoming famed for his many and inventive descriptions of a woman's breasts. 'She should get them out tonight. I'd love to see James McAvoy's, too.'

Indeed, his descriptions of some of the breasts he was confronted with became increasingly entertaining: 'Look at those bad boys!' was one typical rejoinder, and to a woman who wasn't wearing the right bra, 'Those beasts are not caged.' On another occasion he was asked what was his favourite part of a woman's body. 'Tits!' he cried. 'My favourite part of a woman's body are the hooters. I love getting my hands on them. I love getting my face in there, I love dressing them. I love boobs!' There was no other presenter on television, stylist or otherwise, who could possibly have got away with that comment. But the fact that Gok was so good-natured allowed him a little leeway – that and the fact that his interest in breasts was definitely not sexual.

Meanwhile, *Naked* was still airing, with its increasing number of participants whose lives were being turned around by Gok. The latest was Cindy, 40, a mother-of-three who'd spent so much time running around after the kids she'd forgotten to take care of herself. Like so many of the other women in the show, she'd draped herself in baggy clothing to hide the body she had lost so much confidence in. Gok, as ever, dished out warmth and good advice: by the end of the show Cindy was transformed.

Of course, Gok was interested in the way public figures dressed, as well. Asked who had the best and worse taste in public life, his answer was actually quite diplomatic, in that he certainly didn't offend the showbiz community, although the nation's most senior politician might have felt a little put out. 'Salma Hayek usually gets it right and Cameron Diaz looks great dressed casually, but can also pull it off on the red carpet,' he said. 'Penélope Cruz has amazing taste as well.

For the worst, I'd say Gordon Brown because he wears the most ill-fitting suits.'

As the Glasgow gig came nearer, with 2,000 people expected to be in the audience, anticipation was mounting, not least in Gok himself. How many would strip off for him? 'There is no way I will try to get everyone naked,' said Gok (wisely). 'It will be all the fun elements from the show, plus two competition winners getting the full Gok treatment. And some half-naked men in kilts.'

In many ways, Gok was surprised about the continuing fuss about *Naked*. It all seemed so simple to him. 'When you strip the format down, at the beginning you have a woman who doesn't like herself and at the end you have a woman who does like herself. It is really honest, best-friend behaviour. It is good-hearted and we try to make a difference.'

He was absolutely right in that analysis, but the wonder was that no one had ever tried it before. The shadow of Trinny and Susannah still loomed large in the background, along with that of Nicky Hambleton-Jones. Of course, the previous success of their shows had been in part because the viewing audience enjoyed seeing the women involved receive a ticking off, but equally, it was because the three women reeked of the school marm, a powerful figure in the nation's consciousness. It had not, until now, seemed to occur to anyone that an equally popular figure might be the gay best friend.

And then there was the idea of encouragement rather than the barbed remark. Gok, having been bullied as a boy, was particularly sensitive to unpleasantness and had the sense to realise that bracing remarks can very easily turn into cruelty. 'I think the days of bitch TV are over,' he said. 'We don't want to see someone getting slaughtered for wearing the wrong shoes. I don't like this TV dictatorship.' The viewers agreed.

Gok disliked shows that advocated surgery even more, and with some justification. Surgery was surgery with all its inherent risks, and it was a drastic step that should not be viewed as some sort of television game show. It was also telling the subject that they were not good enough as they were, and needed medical intervention to obtain perfection. Gok's way, of taking a woman and making her feel happy about what she had, was clearly much healthier. 'They present the options as: have plastic surgery and be happy, or don't have it and be unhappy,' he said. 'That is so dangerous. It is all about attitude. I don't care if you are wearing Prada or Primark as long as you wear a smile.'

It was a winning way of putting it, but Gok did have enough self-knowledge to realise that he might one day change his mind on a personal basis. Asked if he would ever contemplate surgery himself, he seemed to be taken aback. 'You know what, you're the first person who's ever asked me that!' he said. 'People always ask me my views on it, but not if I'd do it. You never know, I might get to 65 and decide I want to look like the Bride of Wildenstein.'

It was an honest response. Gok was as aware of his own body image as anyone, and by now worked in not one but two industries — fashion and television — that judged people on their appearance and he was canny enough to know he had to stay ahead of the game. But not yet. Gok was a looker and had no need to worry for now.

He was also asked about his own style influences. 'David Bowie, Duran Duran and Bryan Ferry — all for very different looks,' he replied. 'When I was younger I tried to look like Bros. I had Grolsch bottle tops on my Dr Martens and hideous white jeans. I got it down to a T.' It was a long way from the stylish figure he cut now.

Gok, in fact, was the perfect walking, talking advertisement for his own profession, always stylish and immaculate, even if he did favour track suit bottoms when he was at home ('I've got the biggest collection of tracksuits you've ever seen. I look like a glamour girl when I chill out in baggy tracksuit bottoms, Ugg boots and hoodies'). For once, his response when asked if he'd let Trinny and Susannah style him was quite chilly. 'No, because I work hard at what I do and I don't feel that I need a stylist,' he said. Although the question might have seemed innocuous to an outsider, it was an important point in Gok's professional life.

Gok was now fully part of celebrity culture, often to be found in London's media haunts such as the Groucho Club, and in hot demand for other celeb-led events as well. He never failed to give good value, and was always on hand for a quote to amuse. Who, of the famous, would he really like to makeover? His answer came as quite a surprise.

'There are a lot of celebrities I'd like to have a go with,' he said at the London launch of the BlackBerry Woman & Technology Awards at The Hospital. 'I'd like to do Princess Anne. I don't get the horsey thing – I just think she needs a stylist and a bit of updating.' So Gok would like to see the Princess Royal naked? 'I'm not saying that – but yes, I would,' grinned Gok.

If anyone could do it, Gok could, and that's not even taking into account all the celebrities who would have happily submitted themselves to the Gok treatment. Cilla Black, then 64, was one of them and seemed extremely taken with the nation's favourite stylist when Gok went to make her acquaintance. His approach was not the conventional one and would have been totally impossible had he not been gay. 'Gok ran over and introduced himself then asked to take a look at her boobs,' said an onlooker. 'She just yanked down her top. They chatted for ages afterwards.'

Actually, most gay men wouldn't have been able to get away with that either. But such was the force of Gok's sheer charm that he seemed to manage what others never could. Quite apart from the amazing effect he had on the women who appeared on his programme, almost everyone who met him came back from the experience swept away. As his sister said, it might have been because he found it so easy to be physical with people, hugging and embracing people he barely knew, and somehow making them feel important and the centre of attention, that he received such unbounded affection back again. Whatever it was, Gok was almost universally adored.

But he still had his feet on the ground. Gok's success had been sudden and many people who have gone from zero public profile to being recognised everywhere in a short space of time has allowed it to go to his head, but Gok did not. 'Love what you do and never take yourself too seriously,' he advised, when asked about how to be successful. 'Be very thankful for what you've learnt and what you've done today, because it might not be there tomorrow.'

It was sound advice, not just about how to handle fame, but for life generally. Gok still maintained a sense of reality, and thanks to his family, still remained down to earth. While humility is perhaps too strong a word for it, he had sense enough to be grateful for what he had been given, and to appreciate it. There was no diva-like stroppiness. Gok was still very much the boy next door.

# 7
# GOK AND THE GORBALS

*Outgoing Eurasian, 33, London, likes Sambuca shots,* Sex and the City *and slow midnight dances. Seeks like-minded, gorgeous, funny, ambitious, intelligent, arrogant, rich fashionista!*

> Gok's response when asked what he would put in a
>
> personal ad

**G**ok was certainly going down a treat in Scotland. As the live show approached, he was spending time in Glasgow preparing for the show and taking part in all the delights the city had to offer. He was feted north of the border quite as much as he ever had been down south: indeed Glasgow appeared to be welcoming its visitor with open arms, perhaps pleased that this is where Gok was staging his debut stage show.

And the women of Scotland were responding to him in exactly the same way as the women of the rest of Britain.

They absolutely loved him, needed no persuasion at all to shed their clothing for him, felt just as bad about their bodies as the rest of womankind and seemed to see in him a kindred spirit. He understood them. He knew how they felt. It is difficult to imagine a warmer welcome than the one he received north of the border: even for someone who was becoming used to be mobbed wherever he went, this was pretty heady stuff.

Gok, thoroughly enjoying himself, lapped it all up. Used to being the centre of attention everywhere he went by now, he was charming, happy and very pleased to be there. If Scotland flattered him, he flattered it right back, never missing an opportunity to praise his surroundings and say how happy he was to be there. And he clearly was, too. Few people could fail to be seduced by the sheer goodwill he attracted everywhere he went; the sense that here were people who really appreciated him. Was it any wonder that he was so rarely to be seen without a smile on his face?

Part of the secret, of course, was that he was as obsessed by clothes as any of the women he styled, and spoke in their language, too. 'Disaster!' was how he described buying the wrong outfit for a party. Most men would not have felt the world was coming to a halt because of one bad purchase, but Gok did and the women did. And then there was the pleasantness of his manner and his conviction that every woman had a beautiful inner self. It all went down just as well here as it did anywhere else.

But that mischievous streak remained. Gok was, after all,

accustomed to the gay scene in London, and while you can take a man out of the gay scene, you can't take the gay scene out of the man. Among a great deal else, he caused quite a stir when he attended a football match to see Scotland lose to Italy, which caused him to make the usual outrageous comments about the country's football team. 'I discovered a lust for Scotland and its men after finding myself surrounded last weekend,' he said.

'I just love a man in a kilt but some of them really need tips on how to wear them properly. Some of the tartans were fantastic but others were hideous. I would have great fun getting them into kilts with a modern twist. My idea would be a leather kilt with a Hello Kitty sporran and chopsticks stuck down the socks instead of a dagger. The chopsticks would be more useful than the knife because these guys must need good fast Chinese food after watching games at night. Little mirrors on the toecaps of the boots might be fun, so they could see up each others' kilts. I would never get them to wear pants. That's part of their rugged allure.'

The men of Scotland took it well, all the more so when Glasgow's reputation as a hardnosed city was taken into account. As for his take on the kilts they wore, it was so determinedly being cheeky that the reaction it provoked was tolerant amusement rather than anything else. Certainly the idea of Scottish football supporters sporting leather, Hello Kitty sporrans and chopsticks was a novel one, and there were not a lot of people who could have got away with it without attracting derision for their ignorance.

In truth, Glasgow seemed flattered to have Gok in its midst. He brought the limelight with him everywhere he went, and just as women seemed charmed by his attention, so did the cities they lived in. Crowds would turn out in force to greet him, to make him feel as important as he made them. In many ways, Gok resembled nothing so much as a beautiful and exotic butterfly, alighting gracefully and charming all his admirers, before flitting off in search of pastures, and adorers, new. He was nothing quite like any of them had met before, but brought with him the gift of empathy. You knew you could trust Gok.

He was taking part in worthy causes as well, such as attending the annual Action Medical Research Ladies' Lunch at the Glasgow Hilton, where he auctioned off tickets to the show. The publicity machine was hotting up: Gok posed with four models, Iona MacInnes, Natasha Connelly, Lindsay Ewing and Vivien Taylor in Buchanan Street, during which the women, not all stick-thin, stripped down to their underwear. It garnered a huge amount of publicity, both in Glasgow and beyond, and increased the anticipation about what Scotland was about to see live on stage.

In the event, the show was a great success. The Armadillo was packed to the rafters, and the women and the audience loved it. Above all, they loved Gok. It was an important step forward for him, too: he proved he could carry off a live stage show as well as appearing on television. The latter was easier in many ways, not least because one fluffed line could be reshot. Live on stage, it was a different story: not only did you have to get it right first time, but you also had to have the presence to fill out an auditorium, something else you didn't necessarily need in a television studio. Gok had that presence: the strength of his personality was such that he easily carried off being centre-stage – so much so that he managed a Mexican wave in which he got the audience to pull up their tops and show off their breasts in unison.

Ironically, given that Gok was now probably the most famous stylist in the country and that his ability to get close to women stemmed from his relationships with his mother and sister, the women in his family displayed no interest in fashion.

'In terms of my work they influence me hugely, although funnily enough, my mum dresses like a lesbian football player,' he said, rather ungallantly. 'She's not the slightest bit interested in fashion, and neither is my sister, which I think is great. They're inspiring because they're both very confident women, very strong and powerful. At the same time, I'm constantly trying to fix their clothes, although I've pretty much given up on that now. I've taken them both shopping, but they're useless. I'd like to dress them up, but they just won't let me. But then there are millions of things more important than fashion, aren't there? I like that they don't actually think it's all that important.'

His family was, if anything, just as important to Gok now as they were when he was a child. Although his life was now utterly different from his childhood in Leicester, Gok was being subjected to any number of new pressures and tensions that were part and parcel of becoming a well known face.

Quite apart from the hangers-on, the constant scrutiny he was subjected to could have been a heavy burden to bear. It is a testament to his level-headedness that Gok is still not known as a diva in the business, that stories do not circulate about how difficult he is to work with – quite the contrary – and that he didn't let it go to his head. Somehow he managed to cope with it all.

His parents and siblings watched with equanimity as Babe rose from one height of achievement to the next, providing support and a sympathetic ear when he needed it. Gok was behaving with exceptional grace in public, somehow managing to run his new life without any major pitfalls, but as he himself had conceded, it's not always easy being famous, and that strong family back-up was essential when it all got too much.

As for all that female adoration, Gok was gracefully accepting of that. For a gay man, he did spend an awful lot of time with women, but fortunately he liked them – and they certainly liked him. Gok acknowledged as much. 'I do think that I would make a woman a wonderful husband, except that I wouldn't want to have sex with them of course,' he said, rather wryly.

'I just get on so well with women. I think that I have great empathy for them. I understand them to a certain extent, and I genuinely want to listen to what they have to say. I also think that women like having men who aren't at all sexually threatening as friends. That's one of the reasons why women and gay men get on so well.'

Except that plenty don't. On other occasions, Gok acknowledged that there could be some misogyny directed towards women by male clothes designers, but there was nothing of that in his world. Brought up by and surrounded by strong women, his relationship with them was easygoing. He also felt he could understand them in a way that might prove problematic for most men.

'I actually don't think that women are much of a mystery at all,' said Gok. 'That's a myth. If you're genuinely interested in them and in what they have to say, it's all there. I've always been really good at friendship with women – a real love of them. I feel a closeness to them, but not too close! Having said that, I think that there are a handful of women who could probably turn me straight. Gaby Roslin and Diane Keaton are definitely up there.'

That would have had many a female fan wondering, 'What if...' For all that Gok was so obviously gay, for all his campness and flamboyance and sometimes effeminate behaviour, he was a handsome and attractive man who managed to relate to women in a way most men don't. Many women might have treated him like a brother or even as an honorary woman, but it was difficult to escape the conclusion that some of his subjects were a little bit in love with Gok – understandably, given the miracles he wrought with their self-esteem. It has been known for women to fall in love with their doctor because he mends them and makes them whole again, and much the same could be said of Gok.

But for all his pronouncements about being a good

husband, there wasn't much doubt about where Gok's interests really lay. Women were his life's work, but behind the scenes, it was men he spent his time with. His relationship with women, however, was a public manifestation of a private phenomenon, which made its way to the television screens in a dramatised way with *Will and Grace*. Women may love their gay best friends, but sometimes they love them a little bit too much. That was how some fans felt about Gok. However, while he was theirs in some ways, he never could be in others. There was, at the bottom of it all, a barrier they could never cross.

But those were deeper issues. Gok loved his job, which was one of the reasons he was so good at it, and he got to the root of what made it enjoyable. 'Everyone likes to play God, and I think that on a small scale, that's what I get to do when I give a woman a makeover,' he said. 'It's the best feeling in the world to make women feel really good about themselves. I love that women love clothes, and that clothes can really help to bring out their personality. I like to challenge women's perceptions of what is beautiful. Often they can have quite a narrow view of what is attractive. A woman's journey from hating her body to loving it, and loving herself is amazing.'

Coming from anyone else, this might have seemed a little coy. But with Gok, it was all utterly heartfelt. Not only had this been a route he himself had taken, but he was now confronted on almost a daily basis with what he could do for women, and ultimately, at the heart of it all, what he could do was make them happy. And, as he freely admitted, he got something out of it, too. 'Playing God' might seem an extreme way of describing it, but he was in total control of his environment, shaping the women into the way he wanted them to look. Perhaps he was more of a Henry Higgins, the professor who transforms Eliza Doolittle in *My Fair Lady*.

Without wishing to stretch the comparison too far, Gok wasn't just Henry Higgins: he was Eliza Doolittle as well. He might have been his own stylist, his own makeover artist, but Gok had transformed himself just as much as any external person could have done and had learnt his trade on the way there. And now fame, fortune and adulation were his. He was obviously enjoying the material side of success as well, sporting a wardrobe that was more stylish than ever and an increasingly eye catching collection of earrings. But it all added to the show.

Gok was pretty open about it, too. 'Obviously I'm seriously into clothes, and I do have the most varied wardrobe,' he confessed. 'From skater-boy to rock star to mafia-style suited and booted, I'm just constantly shopping so I pretty much have it all. To be completely honest, I have – more than once – been out at a club with friends and decided I hate my outfit, so I've left, grabbed a taxi home to change, then gone back again. It's awful, but there you go.' It was not that dissimilar from the way some of his female subjects behaved, either, something that was equally likely to endear him to his fans.

Gok was, in fact, able to laugh at himself and all the

nonsense that sometimes surrounds clothes. 'I also suffer from a terrible case of wardrobe envy,' he continued. 'I'll be out on the street and see some guy who looks particularly hot and I'll have to find a shop selling what he's got on. Fifty per cent of what I buy is a variation of something I've seen some cute guy in – I'll run to the shop then find a toilet somewhere to put it on!'

He remained, however, as self-deprecating as ever. Not only was fashion not that important, he insisted, but there was nothing particularly special in his approach to the subject either. 'I'm not a psychologist,' he said. 'To be honest, I'm not a very clever person at all. But you don't need qualifications to know what makes people feel crap about themselves.' That was not entirely correct, or if it was, that meant there were a lot of very cruel stylists on television: sometimes people seemed blithely unaware of what made people feel bad about themselves. But what Gok had was empathy and kindness. He knew what had made him feel bad about himself and was very careful not to pass that on to anyone else. And in that care and that concern, the women he looked after adored him even more.

Gok talked a great deal about how much the show changed women, but he recognised that it had also changed him. Being around so many unhappy women and analysing why they felt the way they did also gave him the opportunity to look inwards, and start understanding more about himself.

'I never realised what a rough time I had as a kid until I started working on the show,' he said. 'But suddenly it was obvious — these women were eaten up with the same horrible emotions that I used to have. I have been bullied, I have been fat. I have been an outsider. I have hated looking in the mirror. I honestly believe I have hated myself as much as anyone can. When I tell them that, they seem comforted by it. They know I would never judge them for being fat, because I know how it feels.'

And so he was able to put his experience to good use, and it really worked, too. Although he was right in that fashion is not the most important thing in the world, women are judged as much on their appearance as they always were, if not more. Gok understood that and he understood that appearance played a large part in a person's self respect. 'It's incredible how much better a woman can feel about herself when she changes the way she looks,' he said. 'As a rule, women's attitudes towards their bodies are so out of whack. It's depressing. We've spent too long thinking that beauty is something very narrow, and we're far too wary about what we deem beautiful. I do genuinely think that all women's bodies are really beautiful, and I'd like more women to believe that too.'

This really was extremely unusual, especially coming from a gay man. But although Gok continued to be outrageous, he actually fitted into a very long-standing British role — outrageously camp men have always had a part to play in the national scene. Some of his fans might have been in love with him but others, men as well as women, related to him in a way that was part of the national character. Despite repressive legislation and periods of real persecution, the British have long had a very tolerant psyche and accepted that not everyone was quite the same, even if they didn't go into too much detail about the whole thing.

For there has always been a certain acceptance of that which has been patently obvious but not actually spelled out. Even when homosexuality was illegal, there were figures who strayed perilously close to the line – Kenneth Williams springs to mind – and who were tolerated because, while arch, they posed no obvious threat. The slightly more hardcore gay men, if it's possible to describe them as such – the leather-wearing body builders and the like – have never had such mainstream appeal. They pandered to people's fears about homosexuality, while men like Williams or Larry Grayson merely treated it all as a great big joke.

The same applied to Gok. He might have been totally over the top in his dress, mannerisms and behaviour, but there was absolutely nothing threatening about him because he spent so much time in the company of women telling them how gorgeous they were. It was quite easy to forget the irony of his position – surrounded by adoring women he didn't want to have sex with – while he himself made the odd remark about how we would actually quite like to have a few more men on the scene.

But still Gok refused to take himself too seriously. He was lucky, he knew it and he was taking life as it came. 'I love what I do and I have worked hard to this stage but I know that, without stylists, the world would keep turning,' he said.

'I don't know how long my success will last, but I refuse to panic. I won't bully myself: I've spent too many years being bullied. I don't ever want to feel like that again.'

The world of television is notoriously fickle and there is no way to tell how long Gok could stay at the top, but for now he was certainly a big hit. His attitude, however, was surprisingly down-to-earth, for many bullied children who have gone on to prove themselves in later life retain a life-long fear of having it all taken away from them again. If he shared that, Gok was managing not to say so. He certainly gave every impression of appreciating his good fortune and making the most of it, while not agonising about the future. It was the most sensible attitude a man in his position could take.

And in the background were his parents, slightly bemused by all the fuss surrounding their increasingly famous son, but happy for him. 'They told us to give everything a go and when it all screwed up they were there for us,' Gok said. 'Whether they understand the choices I've made in my life is a different matter. I still think my dad would be over the moon if I said I was opening a Chinese restaurant because that's a proper job in his eyes – but I don't know what I'd do without them.' They were certainly delighted by his success. The family had been aware of the problems that Gok had had as a child, and now here he was, blossoming to such an extent that he'd become the darling of the entire country. It was heady stuff for the family as well as its famous son.

Gok continued to get a real joy out of his work, however, whether styling was important to the world turning or not.

'Women are so much fun to dress,' he said. 'Women's clothes are amazing, and there's so much choice. I love clothes from the really sexy decades, the 1940s nipped-in waist, the hourglass shape of the 1950s. Women's clothes should really celebrate the female form and show it off. I hate seeing it hidden away, partly because I'm jealous of it – I'd love to have a pair of tits for the day! What would I do? I'd probably get them out a lot and have plenty of sex.'

It was hardly surprising that his family were a little taken aback by Gok's world view, but they continued to give him their love and support. At the same time, *Naked* was continuing to air, with the nation as transfixed by what was happening on the screen. Gok seemed to be taking on as many challenges as he could: the next, Debbie, was really an unusual case, for she was a slimming instructor – and one who had lost six stone. She still felt, however, that she had all her old fat-girl insecurities and hated her body. It was Gok to the rescue again. His *How to Look Good Naked* army of 100 consumer testers, meanwhile, were turning their attention to teeth-whitening kits.

Women, as usual, loved it; male television reviewers, as usual, poured scorn. One picked Gok up for yelling, 'Abso-Gok-ing-lutely,' with a dire warning that Gok was in danger of becoming a little big-headed, but no one else seemed to mind. It was these characteristics that the public, or the female side of it, anyway, found endearing. As long as women adored Gok, that was all that really mattered, at least in terms of his career.

But some men really did seem to have a problem with him.

Another was Chris Moyles. When Patsy Kensit appeared on his Radio 1 show, Gok was mentioned and it turned out that Patsy hadn't heard of him. Chris's crew helped: 'He helps women with body issues …'

'Fat old lasses,' said Chris. 'There's some fat bird stuck in a shopping precinct in her knickers and he says, "You look fabulous," and everyone else says, "It's a fat bird in her knickers."' It went to show, though, that not only had Chris heard of him, but that he knew the show as well. If Gok had penetrated into the more macho of the recesses of Radio 1, then it seemed certain he was here to stay.

He continued to be very much in demand elsewhere, too. All About The Dots, a rising Glaswegian punk-pop band, were keen to be styled by the master. 'We met him at his recent SECC [Armadillo] show and this week he told us he will help out,' said singer Jacqui Sinclair. 'We can't wait.' Elsewhere he was spotted at the Family of Courage tribute as well as at *An Audience with Celine Dion*.

Meanwhile letters praising him continued to appear in the national press. And as far as permeating the national consciousness was concerned, so visible and well known had Gok now become that people were referring to 'Gok Wan glasses'. Everyone knew what they meant. Gok had a unique style that made him stand out from a crowd: wherever he went, he was instantly recognisable. Whatever you thought about him, you couldn't ignore him, which was possibly one of the reasons some men (but no women) sometimes found him hard to take.

And there were developments elsewhere. In the continuing Gok v Trinny and Susannah debate, the women themselves had so far not contributed their thoughts. But when they were interviewed in the run-up to Christmas 2007, they showered Gok with praise. Asked about their up-and-coming rivals, Gok and Nicky Hambleton Jones, they were full of praise for Gok, although not for Nicky. 'They only illustrate that there's a demand for this kind of show,' said Susannah. 'I think what Gok Wan does is great, he's very good and handles women with great sensitivity. But, I don't agree with *Ten Years Younger* at all. I don't think people should have to get sliced up to look better. It's too extreme and it doesn't put across a good message.'

'We'd just rather move the theme along into the psychology of individual people, so things don't get stale,' added Trinny.

It was a wise approach to take. The press couldn't resist constant comparisons between the different shows, and while Trinny and Susannah certainly had a legion of admirers, not all of whom had crossed the floor to join Gok's side, they had never inspired the adulation that surrounded Gok. To be snappish about him would be seen to be churlish, to say nothing of sour grapes, just as it would have been in reverse, and so the best and safest line to take was to be complimentary about him. It was an approach that was gracious and would not blow up in their face.

The third series of *Naked* was coming to an end: the last participant was Andrea Perrett, who Gok took through her paces and emerged triumphant. Male television critics continued to gripe, with one complaining that Gok used his own name far too much, as in, 'Thank Gok for my naked testers.' Gok could ignore him: he was undisputed king of the television stylists now. Proof of that was that the public was still writing letters to the newspapers about him, even when he wasn't actually appearing in anything. He had made his way into the national consciousness, and there he intended to stay.

# 8

# A FAMILY MAN

By the turn of the year, it was quite clear that Gok had entered the mainstream. Even people who had never watched a makeover show in their life now knew about Gok Wan. His name cropped up in the most bizarre circumstances, as when one journalist wrote of the inquest into the death of Diana, Princess of Wales: 'It is true that the assessment of the princess in a leopardskin swimsuit by the coroner, Mr Justice Scott Baker, was more evocative of Gok Wan hosting *How to Look Good Naked* than of law in action.' When Gok was cited in those circumstances, it was clear quite how far he'd come.

His family, however, remained the most important aspect of Gok's life and continued to keep his feet on the ground. Interest in Gok and his clan continued unabated, and Gok was happy to explain the dynamics of the family that meant so much to him. 'We don't really have boundaries in our family,' he said. 'I will tell Oilen if I think she looks hideous, and the other day she told me I have the most humungous head. Other people probably find this offensive, but it's all done in love. When we all get together we don't need anyone else around.'

Indeed, the family worked so well as a self-contained unit that other people sometimes seemed superfluous. 'Visitors are sometimes a bit of an intrusion,' said Gok. 'Because we care so much about each other, our method of communication is absolutely crap. We scream and shout all the time, but when we've calmed down we'll all sit and laugh about what we've just done. It's incredibly empowering. I know I never need to worry about pissing Oilen off by overstepping the mark. I don't even think there's a mark we could ever step over.'

A great deal of this was as a result of the difficult times the family had gone through when Gok was a child. All of them had experienced difficulty in one way or another, and their reaction was to band together, to turn inwards into a very strong unit that could deal with problems coming in from outside. The strength of that unit had far outlasted the original problems, and the family remained extremely close.

However, this was to have another, unexpected, angle to it. Because there were so few boundaries with his family, Gok sometimes forgot that the same didn't apply to everyone else. His totally OTT behaviour at home was repeated on the set and elsewhere, and although most people took it in good heart, it was soon to have some unfortunate repercussions. Gok was a larger than life personality but despite his popularity, not everyone adored him. There were to be a few raised eyebrows from some women on the show when they perceived he had gone too far.

But that was still to come and the vast majority of people continued to respond well to his charm – above all the people with whom he'd grown up. Indeed, according to his sister Oilen, Gok was one of the reasons that the family itself all continued to get on so well. Gok had not changed, and she still saw in the stylist-cum-star exactly the qualities she had seen when he was a child.

'We still laugh about the same stupid things we laughed about as kids,' she said. 'Babe loves to throw his arms round people, whether he knows them or not, and because it's meant so warmly they like it. He flings his arms round Mum and Dad and my brother, who is this macho martial-arts instructor. And he cuddles me – he's the only person who does, because I'm not a cuddly person. There's never any awkwardness with him – it's spontaneous and natural. He sits on the sofa, puts his arms around me and rests his head on my shoulder. He's like a spot of glue – he's the physical link that binds us all together.' Her warmth in speaking about him matched that her brother displayed to the rest of the world. Some people have doubted whether Gok could really be as nice as he appeared, but those words of tribute from his sister – and a sibling is sometimes the harshest judge of all – would suggest that what you saw really was what you got.

But Gok retained a very sensitive streak. He had been bullied as a child, and his sister was now a childcare solicitor. She thus dealt with children who had also had a horrible time in one way or another and Gok couldn't always face hearing the details of what his sister dealt with. 'He doesn't like hearing what I do,' said Oilen. 'If I try to engage him in conversation about the horrible things I've seen and heard as a childcare solicitor, he can't face it. He's not that different to everyone else in that respect. Nobody wants to face the fact that not too far from where you're sitting comfortably in your own home a child is being serially abused.

'I don't need him to understand, but I do have a desire for this aspect of life to be acknowledged. The world of celebrity is make-believe; Babe and I manage to happily exist in a world that is somewhere in between.' It was a sign of their closeness that they were able to do so. Indeed, their worlds couldn't have been farther removed from one another, and yet still the entire family remained so close. But Oilen's words about the world of showbiz also hinted at a steely aspect to her character, one which Gok clearly respected. Again, it gave a clue about why he did get on with women: those closest to him were not afraid to stand up and tell him what they thought.

And there was no one Gok was closer to than his mother. He adored her, saw her as much as possible and tried to make her part of his new life. Indeed, she even saw how the shows were made. 'She comes to lots of my filming days and watches the shows religiously, telling me what she likes and doesn't like,' Gok told one interviewer. 'She's my best critic. She does take 20 minutes to tell you what could be said in 10 and when I'm in a rush it can drive me mad. But I feel out of sorts when I'm not in regular contact with her. This week, for instance, I've been manically busy and yesterday I felt really low all day for no apparent reason. I couldn't wait to get home to phone my mum, who I hadn't spoken to properly for two weeks. We talked for over two hours and all in my world was great again; that's the effect she has on me. I hope I've inherited all of her good qualities: I like nothing better than being told I'm like my mum.'

Gok was certainly happy to share his opinions about his world, that of clothes and styling and shopping. 'When it comes to the shops I like, it depends on what I've had for breakfast and the way the wind's blowing at that moment,' he said. 'One day I can spend five hours in Topshop and love everything, the next day I can't stand anything in there – it's completely impulsive.'

As plans began to be made about *Naked*'s next series – television bosses wanted him back on the screen as soon as possible – he found himself again trying to explain what it was that he actually did. Yes, he cheered women up and boosted their self esteem, but some people felt he was now taking attention away from the women's personalities by dressing them in pretty clothes. That wasn't it at all: Gok was allowing women to see themselves as they could be, not covering themselves up.

'It's not about replacing who you are with what you wear;

quite the opposite,' he said. 'It's about using what you wear to reflect and enhance who you are inside. I went through such terrible bullying as a child that I learnt to combat the bullies by focusing on my personality. I'm not about dressing bodies – I'm about dressing personalities. I draw from my experiences when I'm choosing what to wear myself. It can totally depend on where I've been the day before or what I've seen earlier that morning.'

So Gok was now on the receiving end of constant attention, both in terms of his personality and what he wore. He acknowledged that: not only was he famous because he appeared regularly on television, but he was famous because he appeared on a show that was all about appearance – and one that got women to undress, as well.

'There's no chance of being invisible when you're involved in something like *How to Look Good Naked*,' said Gok. 'I do get a huge amount of attention everywhere I go now; women come up to me and some want a chat and others just want to touch me. There's nothing I hate more than rudeness so I would never want to tell someone to fuck off. But it does mean it takes quite a while to get down Oxford Street!'

The fact that they wanted to touch him even brought to mind very much older rituals – it is people who are believed to have healing powers that people want to touch and be touched by. And in a way, Gok did have healing powers. He was healing bruised egos and damaged personalities. He was making the women feel whole again, and that informed his entire life philosophy. 'People should be kind to each other and if you're comfortable with yourself, that comes naturally,' he said. 'All my life people have been making up their mind about who I am before ever finding out who I really am, but I don't need to worry about that now. The only person I really need to please is me.'

Materially Gok was much better off, and he was doing what he loved to do. Moreover, he was doing it in front of an audience of millions, and making himself a much loved figure in the process. If there was a spring in Gok's step, it was hardly surprising: he'd made it, proved his detractors wrong and was hugely enjoying himself into the bargain. 'I would like to do a revamp of a soap,' he said. 'In America, they are impeccably dressed. Over here they all wear the most awful clothes. I would like to get down and dirty with them and make them look like Hollywood starlets.' What the cast of *Coronation Street* thought about that is not known.

But his energy and enthusiasm continued to delight. Sometimes when people have become very famous very quickly, they either turn on the public who has supported them, or blame the media for charting their every move. That did not happen with Gok. He continued to appreciate his huge good fortune, made an effort to make the people around him feel special and delighted in what he did. He was a fund of new ideas, too, constantly thinking about where he could go next with the show and what they should be doing. This was important: if he were to have a long-term career in television, he had to be able to grow and adapt. He'd had a superb run so far – but he'd still only been fronting his own programme for a short time.

In April 2008, the fourth series of *Naked* began to air. It was only two years since the original show had gone out, yet Gok's world had changed totally. Then he was an unknown quantity: now he was an undisputed star. Even so, he was no different with the participants: he was as positive and encouraging as ever, while making each woman the particular recipient of Gok's charm.

Even male critics were beginning to get the point: the new series kicked off with Jeannie, a 29-year-old woman who'd had three children, loathed her stretch marks and kept comparing herself to her identical twin sister, a successful woman called Suzie. Gok suggested she learn to think of her marks as her 'lady lines', possibly their best description yet. The comparison between the two twins was a first for the show, but it was a successful one, while Gok's treatment of the pair of them, especially Jeannie, won him more applause.

One male critic noted approvingly that Gok was actually a lot more sensible than his appearance suggested, telling his subject to stop comparing herself to her sister, start wiggling and get rid of her hideous underwear. 'Mince down there, dear,' he said as she set off on her way down Debenhams main aisle. As for the sisters, Gok suggested, 'we hug each other till we fart.' It was one way of looking at getting the two to get on.

Of course, the show had to evolve to keep people interested. It introduced a new segment called 'Naked

Britain' to get whole groups of people to strip off. 'We tried to get as many people naked as possible,' said Gok guilelessly, adding of his subjects, 'They're desperate for help. It could be Mr Blobby helping them and they would be happy with that.' He got a Weight Watchers group to pose for a picture, too, along with enlisting the help of journalists Rebecca Wilcox and Carole Machin to help the country turn into a nation of savvy shoppers. One critic wrote of his ability to persuade women to disrobe, 'the desperately charming, impeccably dressed Gok Wan, a man whose powers of persuasion have an almost sinister success rate.'

The new series was featured in quite a few newspapers' 'Pick of the Day' slot, with attention increasingly focused on its star. Until now, Gok had been accorded the treatment of a B-list celebrity, but he was now moving fast towards the A-list and people were beginning to give him more respect. Caitlin Moran in *The Times* wrote, 'For now we have the vote, and equal rights legislation, it might well be that Gok Wan, star of *How to Look Good Naked*, is the most significant person in the lives of 21st-century women. I don't wish to overstate his importance, but if Gok asked me to give up my job, and join him in wandering from village to village, preaching and changing the lives of the many, I would. I am an Apostle of Gok ... Gok spends an hour a week getting as many average, thirty-and-forty-something women to take their clothes off as possible. This is an act which provides this country with its sole source of positive, normal female body-images.'

As if to prove the point, the next to appear on the show

was a nurse from Rotherham called Rachel, who was heading for 40, felt fat and frumpy, and thought she was so tall she looked like a bloke. She hated her body so much, she said, that it made her, 'want to vomit'. Gok performed his usual magic in his usual unusual way: he tossed knickers in her face and danced with her in a car park. 'We're all sisters!' he cried. Meanwhile, Rebecca and Carole tested out hair shiners. Everyone loved it, including Dorothy Perkins, which announced Gok was to be its new style guru. Nicki, who hated her tummy, was next.

The show wasn't just making a star of Gok: his undercover reporters were also beginning to attract notice. Rebecca, the daughter of Esther Rantzen and Desmond Wilcox, was one, and the show was perfect for her. 'I am a complete addict when it comes to beauty products,' she said. 'I have got boxes and boxes of them and, when we recently moved house, my boyfriend looked at me as if I was a complete freak because I had so many.' Rebecca had been with her boyfriend Jim for seven years.

Of course, this was the sort of stuff she'd been brought up with: when she was young her mother had headed the team on the consumer programme *That's Life*. And an addiction to lotions and potions meant she certainly knew her stuff. 'I have been playing with wrinkle creams since I was 12,' she said. 'I know it is ridiculous but I love them. If I was a millionaire, I'd drown myself in Creme de la Mer. It's so exciting doing the show and we get to road-test the products. I have got to give up trying to look good, though, as we are put under extreme circumstances – such as the water park to test out a waterproof eye shadow.'

Strangely, due to the vagaries of the filming schedule, Rebecca had not actually met Gok. She was, however, very keen to do so and seemed to have fallen under his spell as much as any woman he met. 'Isn't he so lovely?' she asked. 'I really want to meet him. I'd say no, I wouldn't strip naked but I am sure he could persuade me. Gok has got a brilliant touch when it comes to helping women feel fabulous.' It was what almost everyone who had ever encountered him agreed on.

Rebecca's mother Esther had come in for a good deal of scrutiny over the years, which meant her daughter was well aware how difficult it could be to be constantly judged on appearances. 'It is so much harder for women,' she said. 'Mum is so level-headed but it's still not very nice. I know I am never going to be stunning. But my take is that I am using my brain more, rather than my looks.'

Like so many women, Rebecca had a tendency to put her own appearance down. 'I am gym phobic,' she said. 'I love Davina's fitness video and I have got the comfort-eating genes in me. I love my bagels a lot but if I want to stay under a size 20, I can't go near them.' And if, like her mother, she wanted a long term career in television, she had to keep herself under strict control, too. The cameras add pounds – something else Gok's subjects had to cope with – and Rebecca knew that if she was to become a screen regular she had to be as firm with herself as, say, Gok.

As for Esther, she was delighted for her child. 'She loves the show, too, and she is really proud of me,' said Rebecca. 'We are very close and we see each other at least once, if not twice, a week. She is a fantastic mum. I was a hideous teenager, though. I was the stroppiest cow and I have put myself off having children, I was so horrid.' On *Naked*, however, like its host, Rebecca was charm itself.

In the spring of 2008, however, there was a shock for Gok and everyone associated with *Naked*. His sympathetic approach to women was by now a given, but his language could be ribald, to put it mildly, and to everyone's surprise, one of the participants on the show took it very much to heart. Daisy Idwal Jones, a 25-year-old model who had taken part in a programme filmed at Manchester's Trafford Centre a year previously, painted a very different picture of Gok from the one the nation had taken to heart. According to her, Gok was crude and unkind and she didn't mince her words.

'Gok reduced me to tears on many occasions during filming,' she said. 'I've never been at the receiving end of such vile, misogynistic language and I was horrified. And it wasn't just me. He verbally abused all the models, and even made disgusting comments about our genitals.'

Reading between the lines, what might have happened was this. Gok, as his army of fans knew, was not only extremely flamboyant, but his language and actions were totally over the top. Hence the vast number of expressions he used to describe women's breasts; hence his frequent vulgarity; hence his behaviour which might seem coarse coming from

anyone else, but was meant in genuine good part from him.
Most women saw this for what it was: little more than horse
play, and designed to shock, just as a child will often try to
shock. But the good humour behind it meant it wasn't meant
to be taken seriously, and most women didn't. But in this
case, a couple of people did.

"Gok didn't seem to care in the slightest what he called
us," said Daisy, a plus-size model. "It was disgusting and he
left me with my confidence badly shaken. I don't think
people who behave as he does should be on the payroll of a
national broadcaster. Is this kind of misogyny really
appropriate in a programme that claims to be helping
women to feel good about themselves? What kind of
explanation or justification could there be?"

It should be said that Daisy was not just speaking to a
newspaper about this: she and another, unnamed model,
wrote to Channel 4 and Maverick, which made the show, to
make her feelings known. But it was a very unusual case. By
this time Gok had dealt with an awful lot of women, none of
whom had felt they had the same experience. In this case, the
women possibly took to heart that which was never meant to
be taken to heart. Had Gok really disliked women and set
out to upset them, he would never have been able to
cultivate the image he did – none of the other makeover
television stars were spoken of in anything like the same way
as Gok. He was a hero to the nation's women, not a heel.

So what was Daisy's actual complaint? Daisy said she had
been approached to take part in the show. "They said they

were looking for catwalk models for the series, to flank the ordinary women as they reached the end of their journey with Gok and had to model underwear," she said. "There were eight women taking part in all, and I was booked over one weekend to film the catwalk shows of the first four. The other four would film their catwalk shows at a later date. The fee was dreadful — £300 for three full days' work, which is very poor by modelling standards — but I said I'd do it for free if need be because I thought it was a positive project.'

However, the experience was very different from what Daisy thought it would be. 'I turned up there thinking Gok actually cares about these women and he is here to make women feel better about themselves, but within a few hours, he'd called the other models and me variously a "slag", a "slut" and "dirty little sluts". There was no apparent reason for this language. It was just the names he called us to get our attention, or when he was directing us during rehearsals.

'He also used language that was sexually threatening. He said things like "I'm going to fuck you," which was presumably supposed to be amusing. This was in front of various producers and executive producers from the production company, Maverick. They just all stood around laughing and no one told him to tone down his language or his attitude. It was as though just because he's a celebrity it was OK for him to call us whores. They were condoning his behaviour by laughing with him and at us.'

They probably weren't, but it was the way Gok and his crew behaved. It was a rumbustious crew, while Gok himself went over the top so regularly that he could not have imagined someone was taking it seriously. But Daisy did. Indeed, she began to get increasingly upset by the whole experience, believing she and the other girls were being badly treated. Matters were made worse when she and the other girls were filmed as they were getting dressed.

'I hadn't expected to be filmed at any time other than when I was on the catwalk,' she said. 'But while the models and I were all naked, or topless and wearing tiny G-strings, the camera crew just burst into the changing room and started filming us. I told them I was furious with them, but they didn't stop. I had not given any consent to be filmed naked – at one point the camera was so close it actually touched my body. When I told the producer how unhappy I was at being filmed in such a manner, I was told it would "make great TV". But I'm not a reality TV star – I was employed as a professional, and appearing naked on television is something I would never do.'

In many ways, it was clearly a dreadful misunderstanding. After all, this was a show in which women were encouraged to show themselves naked, or at the very least scantily clad, but it was possible this simply had not been made clear to Daisy and the other woman. As for Gok himself, given the ease with which he usually had women shedding their apparel around him, he, too, didn't realise some of the participants were getting increasingly upset. That being the case, he didn't realise it might be an idea to cool matters down: instead, alas, they got even worse.

'I'd just come backstage from being on the catwalk in front of 2,000 people to face this incomprehensible abuse and people from the production company were just standing there laughing,' said Daisy. 'I felt very upset and extremely self-conscious. My opinion of Gok reached its lowest point. I'd felt like walking out from the first day of filming, and the only reason I'd stayed was because of the contributors. This was their moment and they were dependent on the models for confidence. I didn't want to let them down.'

Ultimately Daisy felt strongly enough about it not only to refuse her fee, but to have all the footage of her removed from the show. It had been a bad experience for her, one she wanted to put behind her and so, very unusually for someone who appeared on *Naked*, she decided not to go ahead with it at all.

'Afterwards, I was very upset and shaken by my experience,' she said. 'I couldn't sleep at all because I was in such a state and I was crying a lot, which is completely out of character for me. I just felt really humiliated by the whole thing and my confidence had taken a very bad knock. After the comments Gok made, I knew it would be a long time before I felt comfortable being seen in underwear again. I have always felt confident and sexy about my body. Suddenly I felt insecure and depressed.

'Within 24 hours of finishing, I'd decided I didn't want to be involved in a programme like that at all. I refused to sign the consent form that I was presented with once filming was complete. I'd entered into a professional engagement in good faith. But it seemed difficult to get anyone to reassure me that I would not appear, against my will, in the final version of the show. Maverick wrote back to me, apologising "unreservedly" for Gok's "unacceptable behaviour" while Channel 4 said that he had indeed been "impolite".'

Rather belatedly, Gok himself became involved. Complaining was one thing but refusing to take part in his show was another, and he clearly realised that whatever his intentions had been, matters had got out of hand as far as Daisy was concerned. Ultimately, he sent her an email. 'I have always expressed myself through my brash and crude sense of humour, something until now I considered unique and funny,' it read. 'I am deeply sorry you did not find this amusing and I only wish I had been more perceptive and I had not been as crude in your presence.'

This was a pretty charming apology, although Daisy went on to complain about it, too. However, it must be said that when the article containing her criticisms was posted online, it attracted a number of comments from people who knew Gok. They were adamant that it had all been a misunderstanding, and that while he might be ribald, Gok didn't have a woman-hating bone in his body. The general consensus was that Daisy had taken personally that which was in no way meant personally.

That was the only public comment Gok ever made about the case. He was deeply upset about the whole affair and said so. Asked about it some months later, he replied, 'I haven't given a response yet because there isn't one. I was absolutely gutted when I read it and that's all I can say about it.'

Given Gok's tendency to push matters as far as they could go, the surprise was that this had never happened before. But the fact that it hadn't did suggest that the vast majority of women did not take his teasing to heart and realised all the OTT behaviour was a joke against himself as much as anyone else.

Gok didn't brood about it either. After all, he was now the most popular man on television, despite the odd hiccup. And he still had further heights to climb.

# 9
# GURU GOK

**G**ok was going from strength to strength. By now he was seen as the guru of all things appearance related, so when a survey came out claiming that millions of women hate their looks so much they refused to leave the house or go to work, he was, of course, asked what he thought. 'I would love it if women everywhere felt good about themselves, but sadly, as these figures illustrate, most don't,' he said. 'It's time for real women to fight back – beauty comes in every shape and size. Women need tools to build confidence and change negative thinking once and for all.'

Dr David Ashton, medical director of Healthier Weight Centres, agreed with him and pointed out that the problem could become very serious indeed. 'Women are under pressure to conform to a norm in society,' he said. 'Even if they are a few pounds overweight they perceive themselves to be massively overweight and they can't face people. That social isolation then leads to depression, which leads to low esteem and the vicious cycle continues.'

The survey had been commissioned by Tesco, who enlisted Gok to help drive the message home. The survey had been done to persuade more women to take part in Cancer Research UK's Race for Life, the largest women-only fund-raising event in the UK, and was now establishing S-Team, to advise women how to look and feel good when exercising. Gok was to front S-Team himself.

Indeed, he was being asked to do a lot of charity work, including supporting Cancer Research's Race For Life. How, he was asked, did he exercise himself? 'Shopping,' replied Gok. 'My cardiovascular exercise comes from the Selfridges sale. When I'm not filming, I go to the gym once or twice a week, I've got a personal trainer and the bastard gets paid even when I'm not doing anything. I walk a lot, too. I've always hated exercise, so it's about finding ways to incorporate it into your life without you realising it's there.'

It was a very pragmatic approach, but then, Gok was a very pragmatic person. He'd had some very sticky times in the past, and it was helping him to maintain a common sense approach to life now. Asked what the best bit of advice he'd ever been given was, he replied, '"It will not always be a smooth ride." I'm quite optimistic and I see the good in everything and sometimes that can be quite dangerous. But knowing things don't always go according to plan helps me out sometimes.'

Rumours of rivalry with Trinny and Susannah, meanwhile, refused to go away. Both sides played it down, but the difference in the way they went about their work was obvious for all to see. Gok trod carefully. 'I'm not sure if people prefer my approach, but maybe some people prefer the format of the programme because it's focused on the relationship developing between me and the person taking part,' he said. 'Everything is real, nothing is staged. When the show ends, you actually care about the person because you know all about them.'

He was becoming increasingly open about what he liked in a man, too. Asked if his heart had ever been broken, he replied, 'Every day, about 10 times! I give a lot and my heart is very much on my sleeve. People pick up on that, which makes me quite vulnerable, really.' And did he believe in love at first sight? 'Yes, I fall in love every day – about 10 times!' said Gok. 'I'm very liberated in my opinions on sexuality and love, my mum taught me that. My parents got together in the 1950s – my dad is Chinese and my mum is English – and when they got together they faced massive problems because it was an inter-racial relationship. But if you love someone it doesn't matter what stands in the way, you should always follow your heart.'

He was right: his parents' story was a touching one, for all the difficulties they had endured, and it had clearly rubbed off on their youngest child. Indeed, according to Gok himself, he was quite the romantic. He was as enthusiastic discussing his relationships as he was at dressing the women of the world. 'I'm a real kid in a lot of ways and I think romance can be a real childish trait – you dream of certain things when you're younger,' he said. 'Some people grow out of that but I love it all. My dates are the best ever, I put a lot of effort into them.'

As for the men themselves, Gok was open about that, too. 'I have a weakness for men in tracksuits,' he said. 'I absolutely love the relaxed, casual, don't give a fuck about what you're wearing look. I spend my whole life making people look pretty and glossy, so sometimes it's nice to see people in a tracksuit.'

Of course, one of the reasons Gok remained so popular was his constant ability to laugh at himself. That first day's work in Habitat all those years ago continued to raise its head and he managed to get a laugh out of it every time. 'A few years ago I woke up and thought, I'm going wear beige today,' he said. 'I put on a beige roll-neck jumper, a pair of beige shoes, beige trousers and a beige jacket. I was working at a furniture store at the time and everyone laughed at me – I looked like the interior of a Ford Cortina. It was the most hideous outfit I've ever worn and my best friends still take the mickey to this day.'

He also was engagingly open about his new life. Asked if he'd ever been star-struck, he replied, 'Yes, several times. I was in the audience of *Strictly Come Dancing* last series and I got star-struck by Linda Henry, who was in *Bad Girls*. She's also in my favourite film, *Beautiful Thing*. I got star-struck by Victoria Wood, too – she came up to me and told me she loved the show. I didn't know what to say.' In other words, for all that Gok was now a star himself and lived in the world of celebrity, he hadn't changed. He was still one of us – the man on the street.

Nor was he going to be tripped up by believing his own publicity. Asked if he'd ever said, 'Don't you know who I am?' he replied, 'Lots of times, but always in jest. I wouldn't have the balls to say it really. I don't think I'm famous enough. Although sometimes I feel like I'd like to say it.'

*Naked* itself remained as popular as ever, and another reason it worked so well is that the production team got on very well with one another. 'I think a lot of the success of the show is down to the off-screen banter, which breaks down boundaries,' said Gok, although he had recently seen that this could also cause problems if he wasn't careful. 'On *Naked* we have this incredibly tight production unit and we get on really well. The women who are taken on the journey are automatically a part of that group. I feel I'm doing something good. I hope I'm changing people's lives and I care about that.'

People continued to be amazed by the success of *Naked*, yet it really was not difficult to tell why it was so popular. It remained a breath of fresh air. 'I offer these women solutions other than plastic surgery or dieting and help them become comfortable with the way they are,' said Gok. 'That's not to say I'm against surgery or eating healthily, I'm just showing my ladies an alternative. You really can look good without going under the knife. Plus everyone loves to watch a good love story unfold and this is what this programme is about – each woman falls in love with herself. It's a little bit of fantasy.'

It was one that Gok was eminently qualified to see through. 'These are real women who have real body issues and I try to help them with their demons,' said Gok. 'They're women who have the same day-to-day problems as the rest of us. I sometimes turn up at their home and they've been arguing with their boyfriend or they don't like the filming and it can get really tough for them. Because I spend a lot of time with them we form a great bond and I still feel very close to all the women I've worked with.'

And his own life was as different from the old days as it was possible to be. 'Going out food shopping is like going to a party,' he said. 'I get people coming up to me saying, "How's your mum?" It's phenomenal. People got wind of the fact that I'm single and since then I've had a lot of blind-date offers. Everyone seems keen to set me up with their gay best friend. That never happened before I was on television.'

Gok was, however, fairly confident about himself. Long gone were the days when he hated himself as an overweight man: these days he was attractive and he knew it. He didn't bother with false modesty, either. Asked to rate his looks out of 10, he replied, 'Eight. I'm quite confident about how I look. I'm quite unusual looking, and I like that. I'm quirky. I don't think I'm model beautiful, but I'm unique-looking, so for that reason I will say eight.'

Would that the subjects of his television show thought the

same about themselves. Next up on *Naked* was Claire, 42, a former Miss Southsea, and it was a mark of how remarkably close Gok was able to get to women and how much he made them trust him that he was able to behave in the way he did. Claire hated her 36E breasts, yet not only was Gok able to tell her that her 'bangers' were amazing: he buried his head in her cleavage. No other man on television would have been able to get away with that.

Rebecca and Carole, meanwhile, were checking out lip plumpers. The influence of *Naked* became clear when the programme got 100 women to blind-test a selection of night creams. The two joint winners were Lancôme Paris Renergie Nuit and the much less expensive Aldi Siana Skin Kind Nourishing Anti-Wrinkle Night Cream: sales were forecast to soar, and they did. In an interview some months later, Paul Foley, managing director of Aldi in the UK, was in no doubt who had wrought the magic. 'Gok Wan is now my best friend,' he said. 'We sell more pots of this each day than we sell bananas. Now keeping in stock is the biggest problem.'

Meanwhile, snippets about Gok continued to spill out, the latest being that he owned more than £40,000 worth of spectacles. 'I've got more than 100 pairs, so I had a suitcase made with compartments for them,' he said. 'I dread my prescription changing.'

He also confessed to something of an obsession with film star Ryan Phillippe. Asked who he'd like to meet, he replied, 'Ryan Phillippe. Because he's just fit and gorgeous and he would get it. I'd love to meet SJP [Sarah Jessica Parker]. I love her, she's so gorgeous. *Sex and the City* stylist Patricia Field, too.'

And who would he like to be stuck in a lift with? 'Ryan Phillippe,' said Gok. 'It's very obvious why. I'd like to be stuck with him for about five hours.'

And if he was invisible for the day? 'Hunt out Ryan Phillippe,' continued Gok cheerfully. 'I'd love to be invisible. I would do so much – I'm so voyeuristic and so naughty.'

Next on the show was Kelly Chamberlain, a bride-to-be who had suffered from breast cancer. This was a far more challenging problem than the ones he usually faced. Kelly, 32, had had her left breast removed, and because of the chemotherapy she was forced to endure, also had short hair. She had been left so distraught by this that she had actually postponed her wedding – matters Gok decided to address at the National Wedding Show.

Just about all the participants in *Naked* were brave – they had to be, given that just about all of them loathed their bodies yet ended up showing them, scantily clad, to a host of strangers and to the viewing public in the sitting room. But Kelly really was called upon to show a lot of nerve. Gok got her to pose in her underwear, while he asked visitors to the National Wedding Show what they thought of her figure, before pulling her up on the catwalk. 'You are fabulous!' the audience yelled at Kelly. It was a very moving event. 'We all really enjoyed filming at the National Wedding Show, the catwalk show was fantastic and when I pulled Kelly up there, the crowd was so responsive it made her feel great,' said Gok.

Diplomatic to a fault, Gok would never have openly preferred one woman on the show to another. But Kelly had certainly touched his heart. 'No, I honestly didn't have any favourites,' he said when the series ended. 'I love all the ladies from the shows. However, I did get very close to Kelly Chamberlain, who was diagnosed with breast cancer at 31 and had to cope with the mastectomy of her left breast. It was a really hard journey for her and there were lots of tears – but also lots of laughter.'

Gok followed this by managing to persuade a whole audience to strip naked. Shortly after this he was spotted at the premiere of the play *Fat Pig* by Neil Labute, starring Kris Marshall, about a larger woman who falls for a small man – in other words, a drama totally suited to Gok's work. Ella Smith, who played the larger woman said, 'You can't see who is in the audience once you're on stage, so it was fine.' On Gok's show, however, everyone could see everyone else.

Having been asked the surgery question, Gok had given the matter some thought. Asked if he'd ever have it himself, he replied, 'Not right now. I'm not anti-surgery, I'm anti people being given one option and told they have to look a certain way. I'm quite at one with how I look at the moment. Apart from when I'm tired.'

Trinny and Susannah were in the news again: by now they were presenting *The Great British Body*, which started in June 2008. This culminated in a meeting of the masses upon a hilltop in Sussex, where absolutely everyone, including the two comely presenters, shed their clothing and faced the world without a stitch: commentators observed all style gurus were getting people to take their kit off now.

Kelly Chamberlain's appearance had signalled the last in that series of *Naked* but Channel 4 were clearly intent on keeping Gok on screen for as long as they could. A new show was already underway to take its place, and this one would be featuring celebrities, among them Joan Collins and Geri Halliwell.

In fact, this show was to be quite a departure from anything Gok had done before. Not only was there the celebrity element, but this was to be an exploration of all things fashion, as Gok was keen to explain. 'We have everything from celebrity guests, where we look at their clothes, to road-testing products and then things like "Five of the Best",' he said. 'I also go head-to-head with the best designers in the world and try to recreate the whole, high-end celebrity designer look from the high street because I think we've got the best high street in the world. It's about the accessibility of fashion and about understanding the principles of fashion. I mean, I was brought up watching Jeff and Karen on *The Clothes Show* and *Star Challenge* and they were part of my inspiration for getting into the business.'

But this was to be very much for the woman on the street. 'What we've done differently is to make it completely accessible for people,' Gok continued. 'OK, you do see the designers but what's been nice is to see the celebrities and some of the worst outfits ever, so you realise that they are human. Whatever we're doing we bring it back to the high street. It's not just about those A-listers on the red carpet trying to look fabulous.'

If anything, Gok was playing down the celebrity angle. 'Oh no, I'm the one who's intimidated,' he said. 'I'm still very much off the council estate in Leicester, kind of playing at this whole TV thing. As a fashion stylist I'm very confident, and I've worked with some very big names, but interviewing people is a new ball game for me and I don't really have an interviewing technique – I go a bit tongue-tied and it all comes out, well... Chinese ... None of it is taken too seriously by anyone.'

One interviewer asked him if he'd like to get Jeremy Clarkson on the show – not such a far-fetched idea, as Clarkson had appeared with Trinny and Susannah in the past. 'I would love to get one of the boys and they would probably have no idea of who I am,' said Gok eagerly. 'I could frighten the living daylights out of them. We could probably swap. If they come on our show, then maybe I could go and drive fast cars.'

What about the way Clarkson dressed? 'He would get it,' Gok continued. 'The jeans and jacket are fine but he's going to get it.'

A less appealing prospect for the Gok treatment was portly comedian Johnny Vegas, although Gok himself was confident he could weave his magic there, too. 'I'm sure I could get Johnny naked,' he said. 'It's entirely about confidence first. The clothes are just the trimmings.'

Had he ever had to bite his tongue when he saw people

who dressed really badly? 'I would never tell people that they look horrible,' said Gok reprovingly. 'That's not my style. I'll leave that for other people. But I will tell people they look fabulous. I will always tell someone in the street that I love their hair or great shoes. We don't do that enough in our country. The Americans are very good at it. We all want to hear nice things.'

He was also interested in Kylie Minogue. Kylie had her own stylist, of course, Will Baker, who she famously referred to as her gay husband, but Gok would also like to get his hands on the petite Australian chanteuse. Her period of dressing should be, '1930 to 1950,' he said. 'I'd go feminine mystery. It was an amazing time for women's fashion, because of the power they gained during the war, and Kylie … Kylie's just had her own war, hasn't she? We should go all Sabrina.'

Gok's family remained in the background offering their support. That famed closeness was still very much there, but the difference between all their lives was increasingly bizarre. 'They're very supportive but it's weird,' said Gok. 'They own a chippie in Leicester and they're just normal, Midlands folk. They see the interviews and that but to them it's not me.

'When I go home, I'm still the baby and I get hit on the head for swearing too much. It needs to be that way. We all have our defined roles in our family. They're all coming down to see the show. It will be a long row of Chinese… a bit like a scene from *Tenko*.' He was making light of it, but Gok's increasing ease with the Chinese side of his character was still very much on display.

That devotion to his family even made its way on to his skin. Gok had tattoos of all of them, both siblings and both parents, on half of his right arm, along with another of a bar code. Asked once if it worked (the bar code, that is), he replied, 'Yes. If you scan me I come up as, "Soft Fruit and Sweets".'

He continued to be in demand, now being asked to present an award at Graduate Fashion Week, and women continued to adore him. 'The reaction from fans is amazing,' said Gok. 'I have had women crying their eyes out in front of me, trying to touch me, telling me how I've changed their life. It's like being a rock musician or something.'

But why? 'Clothes talk,' said Gok. 'They tell your story. And we change women's stories – which are sometimes quite unhappy – without plastic surgery, or therapy, or just – with a dress.' He was right. The women he tended to really did come off the show with higher self esteem, and indeed, with a much happier life.

He was well aware himself of his appeal over other stylists, who gave their subjects such a hard time. And while he remained diplomatic, he now felt able to go a little further than he had done in the past. 'Trinny and Susannah – they're like Laurel and Hardy,' he said. 'And Nicky Hambleton-Jones – I met her at an awards ceremony and you know what? She was really, really nice. But I finally thought, "If I hated my body, who would I want to see?" That's the bottom line.'

But he still didn't take himself too seriously. Well aware of his ultra-gay image, he was more than happy to play with people's expectations of what he should do and what he would be like. 'I'd quite like to get a role in *Ultimate Force*,' he said. 'I'd love to be one of those guys who can come into a room and shoot everyone. And I'm going to do a nude photoshoot – but only when someone offers me £1 million to do it. Then I'll start my own charity, to help bullied teenagers, with the money.'

In June, more news started to emerge about the new show. It was to be called *Gok's Fashion Fix* – Gok was now famous enough to warrant having his own name in the title. At the end of every show, the audience was to be shown a really expensive high end outfit and one of Gok's own creation, and told to pick out which was which. This was fashion for the masses, champagne style achieved with beer money, and Gok clearly couldn't wait.

'It's a huge challenge,' he said. 'This is a show for the people about clothes, saying you don't have to be Victoria Beckham to look amazing. You can be Marge from Bolton and still look absolutely sensational. It's the next step after *How to Look Good Naked*. We're saying, let's celebrate fashion, let's get the creative side of it going. I'm going to teach you how to style yourself.'

It was something the women of Britain needed given that, as a nation, style was not necessarily in the genes. 'The trouble in this country is that a lot of women often take an easy escape route of putting on their husband's tracksuit in

*Above*: Gok catches up with Sarah Jessica Parker (*left*) and Cynthia Nixon (*right*) at the British première of *Sex and the City: the Movie* in May 2008

© *Rex Features*

*Below left*: Fooling around at *T4 on the Beach*, Weston-super-Mare, 2008.

© *Rex Features*

*Below right*: Literally! Appearing on *Friday Night with Jonathan Ross* in July 2008.

© *Rex Features*

Specs appeal: Gok judged the Specsavers Celebrity Spectacle Wearer of the Year 2008 award.

Saints and sinners. All Saints singer, Melanie Blatt, was eventually selected as the winner.

*Above*: Gok joined Alan Carr and Justin Lee Collins as the guest host in the sixth series of *The Friday Night Project* in 2008.

© PA Photo

*Below*: Bride or Groom? Gok, Alan and Justin parodied the wedding from *The Graduate* in a hilarious sketch on the show.

© PA Photo

Ding dong: Gok and Alan 'tie the knot'.                    © PA Photos

*Above*: A host of celebrities have appeared on *Gok's Fashion Fix*, including TV presenter Lorraine Kelly (*above*) and R&B star Jamelia (*below*).

© PA Photo

*Above*: 'She rocked up looking amazing,' said Gok, after Joan Collins appeared on the show.
*Below*: Dannii Minogue, of *X Factor* fame, joins Gok on the pink sofa.

Alexa Chung, the former model and TV presenter, said working on *Gok's Fashion Fix* was 'pretty much my dream job'.

that classic "I hate my body" kind of a way,' said Gok. 'I don't think anyone's got the excuse to look terrible. I think every woman has the ability to look great.' He described the show in another way, too: 'It's a bit like *Top Gear* for girls.'

Gok put his money where his mouth was. Although he spent a fortune on clothes, he went for high street brands as much as designer, and proved that it was possible to look very good indeed. 'I collect clothes,' he said. 'For me, they're my art pieces. Where someone else might go out and buy paintings or sculpture, I buy clothes. But equally, if I go into Top Man and buy something I adore for £30, I'll love it just as much as buying something for £3,000.'

One thing was clear: Gok was now earning a lot of money. One by-product of celebrity is cash earned, and he had now been a regular face on television for some years. He might have been a spender, but he could afford to be, too. And besides – for Gok, clothes were work. He had to look well turned out – otherwise it could have had a damaging effect on his career.

But Gok, as ever, was the first to point the finger at himself. 'I don't have a limit on my spending,' he conceded. 'I should do. My accountant wants me to but I don't – I like shopping far too much. I never really look at a price tag, I just buy it. It's me being foolish because, by rights, I should have 25 houses by now, but I don't. I've never been sensible. I'm like a 12-year-old. It's ridiculous, my spending, and every part of my life's like that. But I don't take things too seriously.'

That tendency to overspend was something else that endeared him to the viewers, because that is how so many people who are interested in fashion behave. Gok acted exactly like so many of the people who love clothes: spending too much and not thinking about the future. Had he been po-faced and prudent with his money, he wouldn't have cut half such an appealing figure. But he wasn't. He was as badly behaved as everyone else. As for that, 'I've got to have it' attitude — it was exactly how fashionistas do behave. That was another of the secrets of his success: he was a man of the people. For all his height, feelings of being an outsider and Chinese looks, he really was one of us.

For all the excitement the new show was generating, there were also concerns in some quarters that *Naked* was not going to come back. It had been a hugely popular show, with a fanbase that saw no sign of diminishing, so Gok's band of cheerleaders was very keen indeed to see it back on the screen. '*Naked* will most definitely be back, but I'm not allowed to say when,' he declared, just before the new show was about to begin. 'At the moment I'm doing *Gok's Fashion Fix*, for Channel 4, which is purely about fashion. It's wonderful.'

It was quite a workload to take on, even for someone as energetic as Gok. He was not only working on the television show, but touring up and down the country, doing his bit for charity, making personal appearances, turning up for celebrity events and more. But it was his time, he loved what he did and his energy was fuelling his success.

Asked what he loved most about the job, he replied, 'I love everything about it, all the different aspects from dealing with PRs to presenting, to styling at fashion shoots. I'm a complete workaholic. I'm one of those people who loves to hate work.' It was as well he did. Constant demands were made on his time these days, but Gok was sensible enough to know it might not last. He was making the most of it all along the way.

As anticipation mounted in the run-up to the show, Gok talked about one of its most famous participants, Joan Collins, who was going to appear. Joan was a very Gok person and he clearly adored every minute he was with her. 'I was so star-struck when I met Joan,' he said. 'She rocked up looking amazing. She's almost the same age as my nan, who's an old lady with white hair. But Joan looks like she's about to ravish someone!' She was also more than a match for Gok. A famously witty woman in her own right, Joan knew the business as well as anyone, was a celebrated clotheshorse and was more than capable of holding her own with Gok.

Gok had always had a personality that bordered on the overwhelming, but now that he had become so famous, he could almost be intimidating. That was certainly not the case where Joan was concerned. She started as she meant to go on: 'Joan Collins is just hilarious,' said Gok. 'The funniest woman in the world. She got out of her car, and the first thing she said to me was, "Darling, I knew you'd be wearing more make-up than me." It was probably true that day. I was so nervous about seeing her I was whacking on the bronzer. I was shitting myself.'

The two met up in the South of France, where Joan has a home, and spent an afternoon shopping together in St Tropez. It was quite an experience. 'She out-shopped me,' Gok said. 'I'm a terrible shopper and can end up spending £600 just because I get outfit envy. But Joan can shop! She's really choosy and picky but so amazing. She's everything you want her to be – glamorous yet down to earth, showbiz yet real. She's 75 yet she's 14. She's a contradiction in so many ways, but so warm, generous and kind, and really funny, too.'

It was a perfect screen combination, but more than that, it was a personal thrill for Gok. 'From years of being a stylist and working with celebrities, you can dread meeting them for the first time, because you want them to be nice and not disappoint you,' he said. 'Joan completely lived up to my hopes and expectations. Afterwards she said, "How many of these interviews have you done?" I told her she was my first and she said, "You can't tell, Gok," which was complete rubbish! She's invited me to dinner at her house and I can't wait.'

# 10
# GOK'S FASHION FIX

**G**ok was in the big league now. He'd already achieved fame on the high street – he was mobbed every time he went to the shops – but rubbing shoulders with the likes of Joan Collins was putting him into a whole new A-list league. He'd also been spending some time with Geri Halliwell, who'd let him dig around her old clothes. 'It was just phenomenal to see some of the Spice Girls' old costumes and also some of the new stuff that Roberto Cavalli did for them,' said a thoroughly overexcited Gok.

'From a stylist's point of view, it was the ultimate thrill, especially seeing the Union Jack dress. Geri has sold some stuff for Breast Cancer Care, of which she's a patron, but there was still quite a lot there. Geri has had bad press in the past for her clothes, but she doesn't take it seriously. She's a real comedian when it comes to her wardrobe.'

Rather charmingly, he was still feeling very star-struck. 'I got really drunk the night before I met her because I was so nervous,' he said. 'So when we rocked up to her house, I was feeling like hell, and thought, I'm about to interview a Spice Girl! She's a huge style icon, and there's me, a little old Chinese boy from Leicester. I was so relieved because she was normal. She pokes fun at what she's worn in the past and is very intelligent.'

Gok's increased status was reflected in the calibre of the guests he was having on the new show. Mischa Barton and Kelly Osbourne were both scheduled to appear, along with some of the most famous design names on the high street. 'We've been really lucky,' said Gok. 'The fashion and celebrity industries support the new show. I was really nervous that they would only see me as Gok from *Naked*, but fortunately the years of styling and the amount of work I put in before hand have paid off. So on the show we have Lagerfeld, Chanel, Cavalli, Missoni, Jean Paul Gaultier and, fingers crossed, Vivienne Westwood – my biggest style icon. Every single day I wake up and love her a bit more.'

And he was keen to emphasise that this was to be a very different show from anything he'd done before. 'I'm so excited as it's something different,' he said. 'It's a move away from makeovers. We want to show another side to fashion, like recreating looks on a shoestring. I get to meet stars, but I also had to film in front of a studio audience for the first time. I was so scared!'

Shortly before the show was due to air, however, Gok

showed he was becoming increasingly adept at appearing on screen. He was chosen as guest host of *The Friday Night Project* with Alan Carr and Justin Lee Collins. Gok had been a guest the previous August, when Kim Cattrall had been the guest host, and he had shown he was more than able to adlib.

Sitting cuddled up next to Justin Lee Collins, with whom he appeared to be holding hands over the buzzer, Gok had flirted outrageously. Alan Carr was sitting opposite with Snoop Dogg and at one point the resolutely heterosexual Justin was forced to tell the two of them to stop talking about sex as otherwise he and Gok would end up making out. Gok encouraged them to talk right away. Kim Cattrall then asked, 'What did my aunt do for Ringo Starr?' 'Swallow,' quipped Gok. (The real answer was 'babysit.') Gok and Justin ended up snogging (or looking as if they were doing, anyway) while the resolutely gay Alan Carr obligingly threw a jealous fit.

Now Gok was back on the show, this time in the guest host slot. It was a measure of his popularity that the audience was beside themselves with rapture as Gok posed, for all the world as if he were a model himself, megawatt smile beaming and sporting a silver sequin bowtie, left fetchingly undone. Gok appeared to be growing more handsome as time went on: several years of celebrity had brought a new sheen to him. He was radiant, and more than ready to give it all he got.

He was also outrageous. His appearance coincided with the engagement announcement between the Liberal

Democrat MP Lembit Opik and the Cheeky Girl Gabriella: Gok imagined them in Rome, at the Trevi fountain, as Lembit proposed with the romantic phrase, 'This just ain't gonna suck itself.' There was then a passionate snog between Justin and Gok (or what looked like one, anyway), while a jealous Alan raged, after which the men settled down to chat. Gok described his upbringing, full of coffee mornings with his aunties. 'Did you ask them to get their bangers out?' asked Justin.

'Yes,' Gok said placidly. 'I come from that kind of family.'

It was all good knockabout stuff. Justin motioned to the band, One Night Only, and asked them to reveal their ages: it turned out that the youngest was 17. 'More fresh meat, Gok,' Justin cheerily went on. There then ensued a parody of the penultimate scene in *The Graduate*, when Elaine is about to get married to the wrong person. Gok was the groom, while Alan was the blushing bride. Alan's side of the congregation all had little rabbity teeth, while Gok's was completely naked. The scene culminated with a hysterical Justin calling Alan from a balcony above the church, wearing nothing: 'Now that's what I call how to look good naked!' said the blushing bride.

The audience loved it, and they loved Gok. He read the news with Alan, acting the straight man, before being interviewed again about what he did. Repeating that he wouldn't advocate plastic surgery, Gok said he told his ladies to 'bang on a big old pair of pants and get out there and go disco dancing.' There was a roar of approval in return.

In the next segment, 'Who Knows the Most about the Guest Host', Connie Huq and Joanna Page were guests. Justin spent some time chatting Joanna up, perhaps mindful that his antics with Gok might be misconstrued. 'What does my name mean in Chinese?' asked Gok, to which Justin got a laugh by answering, 'Steve.'

'Trinny and Susannah,' said Connie, to which there was rather a shocked silence. 'Are not as good,' she continued hastily, but it was clear she'd lost the crowd.

'Man who pretends to be gay so he can get women naked,' said Justin.

And so it went on. The flirtation with Alan continued: 'If we did get together, it would be like a convention of Specsavers,' Alan sniffed. Gok's New Year resolution was to… 'Do *Naked* in Iran,' said Justin. To find a husband, was the correct reply.

The show continued with questions from the audience. Does he watch any other makeover shows, Gok was asked. The audience held its breath as Gok plainly thought before answering. 'I used to, but I don't watch any more, as I don't want to cloud my judgement,' he said carefully. 'They do their job, I do my job.' There wasn't too much doubt about who 'they' were. 'I'm amazing,' Gok concluded, and judging from the shrieks in the audience, those present agreed.

Other revelations included the fact that Bros had been such idols in his younger, plump days that he'd put a picture of them on the fridge to stop himself overeating. Then Gok pulled off his piece de resistance. He got various members of the audience to strip off in order to choose the one who would take part in a game show. The evening ended in more hilarity, and clowning around from Justin and Alan. It was all a great success and showed Gok was more than capable of handling himself in an anarchic atmosphere. It hadn't been a night for the faint-hearted, but the audience didn't seem to mind.

Preparations for the new show continued, as did concerns that he was going to turn his back on the show that had made him famous. But this was emphatically not the end of *Naked*. Gok had no intention of walking away from it: this was just another way of exploring what he did best. 'No, I love *Naked*,' he said, when asked if this was to be the end of that show. 'But I've done four series, so I'm doing this as a bit of a holiday. I'm a stylist by trade, so I wanted to use those skills again. I've been surprised by the public reaction [to *Naked*]. Everywhere I go people come up and want to talk about it. I love it. Put me in a room full of people and I'm in my element.'

With the new show Gok was going to have a co-presenter, Alexa Chung, a former model who was also half English and half Chinese. Also like Gok, she was the baby of the family, who'd had years of experience in the fashion industry, in her case through modelling. Again, like Gok, she was pretty down to earth. 'I was willing to look like a bit of an idiot,' she said of her modelling career. 'I was never too precious about the faces I pulled. I did loads of teen magazines and rubbish high-street campaigns.'

Unlike Gok, however, she had become rather disillusioned with the fashion industry and had given up modelling because, she said, she'd developed a distorted body image and low self-esteem. The move had worked: 'I've used up all that neurosis – there's none left,' she said. 'I'd rather have a bigger brain than smaller bones.' Initially she contemplated going on an art foundation or fashion journalism course, before, in January 2008, she was unveiled as the face of Antipodium's Spring/Summer collection and as the face of Oxfam's ethical range. She also modelled for Gok's idol, Vivienne Westwood, something that could only have endeared her to her new friend.

Alexa was not new to television work: indeed, she'd done quite a bit. She had co-presented *Popworld* for a while and appeared opposite Ben Elton in ITV1's *Get a Grip*. She was unfazed by Elton, remarking, 'He'll tell me about Margaret Thatcher and I'll hit him with a few facts about Razorlight.' Various other presenting jobs ensued, including *Big Brother's Big Mouth*, *T4*'s V Festival coverage, various film and music specials and the early morning music programme *Freshly Squeezed*. Along with that, she presented BBC3's *The Wall*, alongside hosting various industry awards, including the Elle Style Awards 2008.

She was also a good match for Gok when it came to her own personal style. She had appeared in various best-dressed lists in 2007, repeating the trick in 2008, when she got into the top 10 in both *Tatler* and *Glamour* magazines. Like Gok, she took inspiration from a wide field. 'I either want to look like an excellently dressed boy or a kitten from the 1960s, like Françoise Hardy,' she said. And, like Gok, she was pretty down to earth about the attention showered on her. 'It's odd to have acquired this style icon tag, because everyone in Shoreditch dresses the same,' she once said.

Unlike Gok, Alexa was known as an It Girl. According to the *Sunday Times* style magazine, she was 'a must-have at any self-respecting fashionable party'. Alexa seemed rather unsure what she thought about that. On one occasion, she remarked, 'I mean, there's not much to being an It Girl. It's really quite a depressing title to hold.' On another though, she was a little more positive. 'It's actually rather nice, because you are sent some pretty cool stuff,' she said.

Already a seasoned professional by her early twenties, Alexa was also very aware of the dangers of overexposure. 'I don't want to shove my face down everyone's throat,' she said. 'I don't want to be famous for going out… It's very difficult if you're in the middle of something to see it clearly and I don't have any idea of what it looks like from the outside or how I'm perceived … I'm sure there'll be some new whippersnapper coming up pretty soon, with a snappy new haircut and wearing Marni and vintage T-shirts.' It was a pretty mature attitude for such a young woman to take.

Alexa was also frequently spoken of as a sex symbol, something else she clearly felt a little uncomfortable with. 'I'm perhaps the least sexy person in the world,' she said. 'I don't want to look sexy in photographs. I think it's an easy option. I'm so sick of girls pushing their boobs up in

MySpace photographs. I hate the way women want to be "hot" all the time.' That said, she was undeniably easy on the eye.

She was also the perfect person to work with Gok. 'Alexa is going to go out there and interview some of the designers,' he said. 'And she's also doing a strand of the show called Road Test, where she'll be road testing different fashion products and she'll be joining me in the studio every week as well.'

Getting the big names involved was not a problem. Gok's reputation was such that it was the stars who wanted to appear with him now, rather than vice versa. 'Actually, we were really lucky,' said Gok. 'The format of the show is brilliant – a lot of celebs are exposed to so many different genres of fashion, but a lot of them never have the opportunity to talk about their own personal style, and how their image has helped their career. I think they've really enjoyed the chance to talk about the clothes they love, so they've all been really, really helpful, and come on the show and had some fun.'

Gok's enthusiasm was palpable. This show was to be quite different from *Naked*, and he was bubbling over with ideas. 'Every week we'll be showcasing the latest "must haves", with all the latest information about the hottest things hitting the shops,' he said. 'We'll do "Five of the Best", each week concentrating on a different type of outfit. So, for instance, the first week is floral dresses, and we'll look at five of the best of them, in different price brackets. We've got the catwalk show, which is absolutely phenomenal, we've got hair, we've got make up. Basically, if you'd been swung around Joan Collins' wardrobe three times and came out of it, that's what we've got on the show.'

That experience with Joan Collins had really hit home. Gok was not that impressed by people just because they were famous – after all, he'd been doing his job for a long time – but Joanie was something else. And it's difficult to imagine a more Gok-type person than Joan Collins: if ever there was a match made in celebrity heaven, this was it.

'She was amazing,' said Gok, sounding as much like an infatuated teenager as he did a sophisticated man about town. 'So much fun. We took her shopping and I was really nervous, but she came out with so many one-liners, and said I was the gayest person she'd ever met in her whole life. I find that quite hard to believe, considering she's Joan Collins and she's probably the gayest person I've ever met in my entire life. Everything she touches turns into a *Dynasty* moment. At one point she dresses me up and tells me I look like a drag queen. She's quite hardcore.'

And unlike so many stars of today, Joanie looked and acted like a big deal. Not for her grunge and no make-up: she harked back to an earlier era, when to be a star meant you existed on a different level from everyone else. 'I loved meeting Joan,' said Gok. 'She is an icon. She is lovely, sweet, she's showbiz and the people she hangs around with … it's amazing. It's Valentino. It's stars and I want to hear that. I don't want to hear her say, "Actually I was down the Spar last night buying a roast chicken." She is so confident and she so knows who she is — she could be wearing a tablecloth and she'd still be still Joan Collins.'

Gok's experience as a stylist was also standing him in good stead. He'd been a working stylist for years before he became famous, which meant he already knew a lot of the big names. He was also used to working with stars, was aware they could be difficult and knew how to handle difficult behaviour. Asked if the stars he had styled in the past had refused to wear the outfits he suggested, the answer was an emphatic yes. 'Every single one of them, at some point,' he said. 'You have the biggest arguments in a fitting, with everybody, whether it's a model or a celeb or whoever. Of course, what I have to do is convince them that they're going to look gorgeous and fabulous and feel wonderful in what I put them in. And that can sometimes take a bit of work.'

Not surprisingly, given the cachet his name now carried in the fashion industry, Gok was working on a clothing range of his own. He was starting small, designing just underwear, but there could be greater things to come. 'I'm really happy with my underwear range, but I'm not confident enough to launch a clothes line just yet,' he said. 'I'm such a control freak I'd have to be completely involved in it, down to the cuts and fabrics and fittings, and I don't have the time. But I've designed costumes for music videos and things like that; we'll have to see.'

It wasn't just the clothing range that was on his mind: both the new television show and his personal life were, too. And he was also beginning to think about how to put his fame towards helping children who had suffered in the same way he did when young. 'I have so many things I want to do,' he said. 'Not only do I want to get married and have kids, I want this show to be a success, to reinvent *Naked* and to do some social documentary TV. Next year I want to open an anti-bullying, fashion-based charity that will help kids in situations of domestic violence and also those being bullied at school. When I was being bullied as a kid I had nowhere to go to and I think it's really important. Hopefully, next year my name will be big enough to do that.'

His name was already pretty big. Gok's has been one of the more meteoric rises to fame in recent times: no one had expected *Naked* to take off in the way it did and no one had expected him to become the star he did. Gok himself was the first to acknowledge this but he was also determined to keep his feet on the ground. 'Everything's changed,' he said. 'Everything and nothing at the same time, because I won't allow it to. Fame comes at a price – you lose your anonymity and people expect you to be a diva. If anything I work harder at not being one. I've had to work harder at things like my friendships and family life as well.

'My mum is my life barometer – she's amazing. The biggest thing, though, is people recognising me. Sometimes, up to 300 people a day ask for pictures and autographs and stuff. Being half Chinese, I stick out in a crowd. I still can't believe everything that's happened. When I rocked up for the first day of filming *Gok's Fashion Fix*, there was a van with my name on it and I screamed, 'Argh! That's my name on the side of that van!' I've been given so much – I have to pinch myself every single day.'

Sometimes his newfound celebrity caused problems, and he wasn't yet experienced enough at being famous to realise that they would. Stars simply can't go out like the anonymous man on the street can: for a start, they risk getting mobbed. At its worst, it can even risk causing danger. 'I was going to the Spice Girls gig last year and I walked into the O2 arena and the whole place erupted,' Gok recalled. 'I thought the girls had come onto the stage and went to sit down but in the end security had to come and take me and my friend out and put us in a box because we'd caused a fire hazard by everyone crowding on the steps to try and get to us.' It was a very different life from the one he'd had before.

On the subject of his rivals Trinny and Susannah, he was ever more succinct. 'I think everybody wants me to have a big mud wrestling match in the middle of Selfridges, but it's not like that,' he said.

With his new show, Gok was now intent on showing British women that they could achieve a good look through high street brands: they didn't need to spend a fortune to look great. 'It's not necessarily about the bargains, it's about putting the clothes together for less,' he explained. 'I get given £200 per outfit, and I have to style the whole outfit, including shoes and accessories, all the customising and everything else. We've got such a strong high street in this country, I think fashion is accessible to everyone. You've only got to walk down Oxford Street to discover that you don't need thousands of pounds to buy a wonderful outfit.'

In another interview he explained it further. 'But the main USP [unique selling point] of the show is that I go up against the big designers,' he explained. 'The idea is to prove to people that you don't have to have a million pounds to feel good about yourself, you can do it on a budget. So what we have is four models who model designer clothes that cost thousands and thousands and then we have another four models modelling outfits that I've put together from the high street for £200 each, from the accessories through to the shoes. Then we have a 'catwalk-off' and the studio audience decides what they like best – and hopefully I win every week!'

And in doing the show, Gok had been going up and down the country, seeking out people from all over Britain, too. That had also been an eye opener. 'It's been great fun actually,' he said. 'We're stopping people and analysing their outfits. It's brilliant, you see so many different flavours, so many different styles, so many different walks of life. It's a real insight into the way people dress. And it's really interesting, I've discovered that geographically people dress differently as well.'

And Britain as a nation was very receptive to fashion. 'I think that we're very fashion savvy,' said Gok. 'We're very disposable. We're quite fickle when it comes to our fashion. I think we dress well. But a lot of our fashion is governed by the climate. I think, on the whole, we get it right, but everyone needs to be Gokked a bit further.'

And he certainly knew how to charm. One of the many locations Gok visited in order to make the show was Liverpool, and he could not have been more effusive, when he was interviewed by a local journalist. 'Liverpool is the fashion Mecca of the north. It's where the best designers in the world look to for inspiration, and this is all about celebrating that fact,' he said. 'When they said we were going round the country I said "We have to go to Liverpool". It's one of my favourite cities ever. I used to be up here all the time clubbing – Liverpool was easier to get to than London when I was growing up, so I'd always be in Cream and Garland's.

'I know people say Liverpool is all about wags and designer labels, but it's not. It's about your own unique brand of style. It's not about expensive price tags, it's all about individuality and not being afraid to stand out in the crowd. The girls last night were looking fabulous. And the boys weren't bad too. People really dress up here, and I love that.' He was in his element in the city, which accorded him an equally warm welcome, and ended up naming Ann-Zoe Ojedapo as Liverpool's most stylish person. So popular had Gok now become that when the programme makers lost touch with the teenager, the *Liverpool Echo* ran an appeal to find her – and indeed, she got in touch.

Indeed, the way in which she was chosen was typical Gok. A catwalk was set up in Williamson Square, and hundreds of hopefuls turned up to stroll down it under Gok's watchful eye. Ann-Zoe just happened to be in town shopping and went over in order to meet Gok, before walking away as the most stylish woman in town. 'Her style is unlike anything I've seen before,' said Gok. 'Her eclectic mix of urban meets emo provokes a luscious combo of true street style. Words that spring to mind to describe her style are genius, fashion savvy, courageous and daring. Britain is known the world over for its street style – it's where the best designers in the world look to for inspiration, and this is all about celebrating that fact. Britain has style like no other country on earth!'

One of the advantages of his growing celebrity, of course, was that like many people in the public eye, Gok was sent free clothes. He enjoyed it, too, but was adamant he also liked to pay his way. 'I'm very lucky,' he said. 'I collect clothes and shop a lot, and people let me have things and I get nice discounts. But not everywhere. And I don't want to be given everything. I'm from a very working class family and I love the idea that if I've worked really hard, whether it's a jacket from Top Man for £40 or a pair of trainers for £1000, if I've worked my arse off, then I want to buy it.'

Gok's appeal to women continued to be a subject of debate, and Gok appeared to be as mystified about it as everyone else. 'I don't know,' he said, when asked why women adored him so much. 'I think it's because I'm really normal. I don't see myself as a celeb, as untouchable, I'm not arrogant or affected by anything, I'm just a working-class, council-estate boy done good. I've had my fair share of shit over the years, to be honest, and I just don't believe in being mean to make you feel good about yourself. It's not that fucking serious, if you think about it. We're sat in a room with a load of muffins chatting about a new TV show. It's not that real, it's not that serious.' It was a very down-to-earth approach that merely served to increase his appeal.

Strangely enough, however, Gok had no desire to work similar magic on men. 'I'm nervous about it,' he said. 'The paunch and man-breasts would be the big problems. I think men are as emotional about their figures as women. In fact, they have a rougher time. Men see talking about their bodies as effeminate or gay, so they bottle it up and feel very isolated with their body issues. Plus they don't have the same kind of tools as women, like magic underwear.'

And it didn't hurt that he was so constantly prepared to poke fun at himself. Had he made any hideous fashion faux pas? he was asked. 'Every single day of my life. You can always guarantee that by tomorrow I'll be appalled by what I'm wearing today,' he replied. And how many times a day did he get changed now? 'Three or four times a day, normally,' said Gok. 'Depending on what I'm doing. I normally have to change my outfits for work. But I always change a minimum of twice, anyway.'

Despairing of his own style was a theme Gok constantly harked back to. In the new show, a segment was to be called, 'What Were You Thinking?' Gok was open about the fact that that most certainly applied to him. 'Everything I've ever worn,' he said. 'I look back at pictures or press shots or shows, and think what was I thinking? But I never take it too seriously because to me, that's not what fashion's about. When I was younger I remember going out, way before bloody Beckham did it, I used to go out in sarongs and big oversized corsages, and costume stuff to go clubbing in. And another time I'd have all my hair braided and a Naf Naf jumpsuit. I love fashion, and the idea of dress-up and costume and playing around.'

How would he react to the live audience on the show? 'I'm bricking myself,' said Gok. 'But it should be fun, it's a real audience participation event. They'll be getting involved and we want their opinions and comments.'

# 11

# LIFE IN A TIME CAPSULE

**W**hen *Gok's Fashion Fix* kicked off it was, as expected, the choice of the day in many newspapers' television slots. Geri Halliwell was on the programme and came up with the goods: she'd had help from some very famous friends to help her update her look after leaving girl power's most famous band. 'Being in the Spice Girls I had been in a time capsule,' she said. 'Then when I moved on, I moved in with George Michael and Kenny. They took me on as a project and re-styled me. I remember the two of them taking me to Barney's in LA and restyling me and putting me in Armani suits. I was going from platform shoes to that and wiping the make-up off. I was like their little doll.'

She was also still the same old Geri, she proclaimed, and showed off an £8.99 pair of gold hotpants, which she wore for her 35th birthday. 'I do like inexpensive,' she said. 'You can take the girl out of Watford, but you can't take Watford out of the girl.'

Gok approved. 'Girlfriend, that's a Gok high five,' he said.

Indeed, Gok continued to rave about the whole Geri experience. 'Geri took me through all her outfits from the Spice Girls tour, which was tremendous,' he said. 'While I was interviewing her, her dog tried to hump me.'

But it was the Joan Collins experience that really thrilled. 'Phenomenal. I mean absolutely phenomenal,' said Gok. 'She's a huge icon. It was scary. I mean, I was absolutely bricking myself, and she could tell as well and she completely played up to that which was so much fun. But in fact she's all warm, kind, generous, fun, really hilarious, very showbizy as well. Which is exactly what you want from Joan and you get it from her. Even though she's been given so many free clothes from big designers over the years, when she does functions and stuff she reinvents what's in her wardrobe already or she designs it and gets somebody to make it. She's 75 years old. I mean, you go girl! I mean, she's brilliant. She takes it very seriously.'

As, of course, did Gok. The new programme featured four 'Gods of Fashion' and one of these was Brix Smith-Start, who owned the Start Boutique chain of shops. 'He is a champion for women. And they just go potty for him!' she said. 'They really do. He's very approachable, very witty and funny and he really does fly the flag for the high street. He's got a real, deep passion for that kind of fashion and clothes. He's not elitist in any way and he really supports the high street – but he also has a great understanding of couture and high design.'

Another reason his approach worked was that he treated everyone the same, whether they were famous or not. 'I never look at a client and think, right – you are this person,' he said. 'I have to give them a consultation and work out exactly what I'm dressing them for. It's like preparing a meal for the Queen or preparing a meal for your mum. It makes no difference. You use the same ingredients.'

As he was giving so many interviews to publicise the show, one interviewer could not resist pointing out that Trinny and Susannah were now stripping off too. Could this be something to do with the Gok effect? Gok's answer was a little less diplomatic than it had been until now. 'Whatever they do is their prerogative,' he said. 'I haven't seen their show and I won't watch it – I don't mind saying that. I won't watch it, because it's just … you know, I love *Naked* and I'm loyal to the brand. They're doing their own thing, they're working – I'm sure they've all got bills to pay.' It was as near as he'd come to being bitchy so far, but then he could now afford to be. He was winning hands down.

And would there be any nudity on the new show? Naturally. 'There's a section of the show called, 'Can You Squeeze Into These?' so you will see some flesh – of course,' said Gok. 'Wherever Gok goes, there's always a bit of flesh.'

However, he was keen to emphasise that the new show was far more about fashion than the *Naked* had been. 'This show is a celebration of clothes,' said Gok. 'Whereas *Naked* was out there at the forefront of body issues, this show is looking at how people are told that they have to have a certain amount of money to look good. This show unveils all of that, saying that you can do it on a budget. A big part of the show is up against the designers but what I'm trying to do is prove that what you can do is you can get that high-end, glossy look and do it on a budget.'

Gok was also asked about what a stylist actually did. He had been doing this for years now, but what did it actually involve other than putting on clothes? Gok was patient in his reply. 'I have to make people feel better about themselves, to get them in a position where they feel confident enough to go up against what they're doing, whether that's a photoshoot or a red-carpet event or an interview,' he said. 'Get them warmed up and feeling good so they perform at their best. It's not just about choosing a pair of shoes.'

That was clear from the show. Gok had taken women with serious problems, such as beating cancer, and shown them how they could make themselves feel so much better by dressing in style. In the new show he was going to try to show all women how to dress. Gok was asked if there was going to be a conflict here: Alexa was set to interview some of the giants of the industry, people such as Karl Lagerfeld and Roberto Cavalli, so would Gok be advising women not to buy designer items as they could get the same look for much less?

'I would never do that,' he declared (and indeed, he couldn't have done if he'd wanted any future in the fashion industry). 'What we would do is celebrate his amazing designs – the designs on the high street have to come from somewhere and they're dictated to from the high-end designers. We celebrate them, but then say that not everyone can afford to have that, even though it's amazing, so let's do it another way.'

And he took teasing that he was the new Selina Scott in his stride. 'I love being the new Selina Scott,' he said. 'I always really fancied her. I'm going to be cheeky enough to say yes it does [make him the new Selina Scott.] There you go: Gok Scott!'

In some ways it was a very apt comparison. Selina Scott had fronted *The Clothes Show*, a forerunner of what Gok was doing. Indeed, Gok had watched the show himself as a child. 'I grew up with *The Clothes Show* and it's how I got into fashion myself,' he said. 'And so I am very honoured to be doing this. I really want to show people that you can do high-end outfits on the high street. As for the celebrities, well, it's so exciting.'

It was an endearing approach. Indeed, Gok was most certainly not taking his new life for granted: he knew how lucky he was, and that he'd been given a great deal. 'If I think about it all, I get scared,' he said. 'I am a realist. I understand what happens. You see people go up, and then reach a plateau. What I have been given is the most amazing opportunity and I just want to enjoy it all while I can."

Indeed, if anything, Gok seemed a bit bemused by it all. According to himself, he had just been lucky to have landed the show. 'Do you know what? I don't see myself as a celebrity at all,' he said. 'I just see myself as Gok from the block. It's not part of my reality. I've worked for so many years behind the camera this is work for me. It's not like I've just left the Big Brother house and suddenly been thrust into the limelight. It's been a bit of hard graft to get here. People say, "Oh you're a celeb", and I kind of know that people know who I am and I kind of see my pictures in the magazines and the papers and stuff. I'm not famous for that. I'm famous for being a stylist. And *Naked* is a much bigger brand than I am.'

On which note, he was keen to reassure the public that *Naked* would indeed be back. '*Naked*'s not gone away at all,' he said. 'I mean that's in redevelopment at the moment. What I don't want to do is I don't want *Naked* to become a show that goes out every single year, looks exactly the same, the same results – people get bored of it. I'm so precious about it. I love it so much, it's such an amazing programme, I want it to go out on a high note. We got the best figures on our fourth season ever. It keeps on going up and up and up, so I want to keep on giving it out to the people and just making it better. So, whilst we're developing that I'm going to do *Fashion Fix*. So it's all good times.'

Gok was now also talking increasingly about starting a charity for children who'd been bullied. 'I want to give something back,' he said. 'I want to do so many things – I want to take over the world!'

That included featuring men on *Naked*. 'I wasn't ready

before,' he said. 'I didn't feel I was confident enough to talk about the brand. But I recently helped Kelly, a woman who had just had a mastectomy, and she gave me the confidence. She had been through a massive struggle, but still walked away with something from the show, and so I'd love to do guys next time around.'

Indeed, at times the experiences could be absolutely overwhelming for the women who came on the show. 'I have had women crying their eyes out in front of me, trying to touch me, telling me how I've changed their life,' said Gok. 'It's like being a rock musician or something. It's like being the Beatles. Clothes talk. They tell your story. And we change women's stories – which are sometimes quite unhappy – without plastic surgery or therapy, but just … a dress.' And it was true. They did.

He couldn't, however, resist bitching about men in the public eye. Attending a summer party in honour of HarperCollins authors at the Victoria & Albert Museum, he quipped, 'William Hague? Well, he doesn't even look good with clothes on, let alone off. Gordon Brown certainly needs a damn good suit. Boris Johnson is my favourite, although he needs a total going-over and style change, which I'd be happy to help with. I think he is a really good-looking guy.'

Gok was still having to cope with people watching him and following him every time he went shopping, but he was beginning to cope with it quite well. 'I shop like a nutter but people do follow me around,' he said. 'If you saw Gordon Ramsay in Sainsbury's with a basket, would you like to see what he was putting in it? Of course! And so when I go in Selfridges or Harvey Nicks, I do have people following me around. It always makes me laugh. I try to go in disguise but what with me being a 6ft 1in Chinese homo, there are not many around.'

It wasn't all fun and games, however. Although he made it look fast and fizzy on screen, in reality Gok worked extremely hard, and it sometimes took its toll. 'I always have a kind of breakdown and halfway through filming a series, I have my own trip out to a counsellor, because I need to lay it all out and get it off my chest,' he said. Of course, Gok acted as a kind of counsellor himself, certainly on *Naked*, and to a lesser extent the new show. He became so personally involved with the women, even if it was only for a short time, that he took a lot of their needs and worries on board. It was hardly surprising that he, too, would need some kind of release mechanism to deal with his own, and others', emotional needs.

The new show was going down well and there had certainly been some thought put into it. Apart from the search for Britain's most stylish person – 'You don't have to be a slave to fashion to be a style icon,' said Gok –there was a sequence in the opening show in which women demonstrated how impractical high heels were by racing around a racetrack in enormous wedges.

When the show started to air, exactly the same divide opened up as before. Female viewers loved it; male reviewers hated it. One pointed out that a show telling you how to dress on a budget included both Roberto Cavalli and Joan Collins; another complained that Gok's high-street clothes were altered by the man himself before being set up against the high-end stuff. But that was the point of what Gok was doing: teaching people how to be innovative. The idea was that you could wear high street and still look individual, something the male critics didn't seem to grasp.

Alexa, who described her role on the show as, 'pretty much my dream job', seemed to be having a little more trouble with being recognised than did Gok. 'When I realised that I was famous, it occurred to me that fame doesn't really exist any more,' she said. 'And then I went to Selfridges and saw Mariah Carey, and realised that it was still very much alive. I don't really want to be recognised for presenting, or for wearing clothes. Also, when you're famous, you have to be polite all day. So when someone asks for your photo, that's the only time they've done it that day, but for me it's the 15th time, and I might say no, and then they'll think I'm a bitch.'

And, of course, working on a show like this, there was a good deal of comment about Alexa's own appearance. She had been angered when *Loaded* dug out some old photographs of her and printed them, looking stunning in pants. 'I don't want to look sexy in photographs,' she said rather irritably. 'I think it's an easy option.'

Gok, meanwhile, continued with his almost uncanny knack of tapping into the female psyche. His latest venture was to turn to *Sex and the City*, putting together outfits that the four women would wear for under £200 each. He also took as his latest celebrity subject Kelly Osbourne. Alexa, meanwhile, interviewed Karl Lagerfeld, and went behind the exceedingly stunning scenes at Chanel.

While the male critics carped, women continued to adore their hero and friend. Lorraine Kelly featured on the show: 'I was out filming with Gok Wan this week for his new series *Gok's Fashion Fix*... Women in London's Oxford Street were throwing themselves at him, some with tears in their eyes,' she wrote. 'The love and adulation was palpable. Unlike most fashionistas, Gok thinks that every woman, no matter what age, shape or size, deserves the chance to buy affordable, stylish clothes and to look her very best.'

She was being generous. Unusually for him, Gok had appeared almost like Susannah and Trinny as they delved through Lorraine's old wardrobe. Pulling out a tartan jacket, Gok declared, 'It's absolutely bloody horrible. It's ghastly.'

'I can't bring myself to throw it away,' said Lorraine. 'I wore it on my very first day at *GMTV*, 14 years ago.'

At this point Gok insisted on modelling it for her.

'Yes, it is horrendous,' conceded Lorraine.

Gok himself was thinking increasingly about the future, and the idea of making over men was clearly appealing. Back on *Jonathan Ross*, he told the host, 'I've done lots of women. Now I wanna do men. So I want to get you in front of those mirrors.'

Back on the show, Gok travelled to Paris with Mischa Barton to go on a shopping trip. Alexa, meanwhile, was off to Milan to investigate the Missoni label. Gok then played host to *X Factor* judge Dannii Minogue, who remarked, 'I was led astray by a couple of drag queens,' while Gok paid her the ultimate compliment. 'I'd turn for you,' he said. Dannii meanwhile, revealed an unusual way of shopping: she licked a £3,000 bag the pair was examining. 'It tastes good,' she explained. Lulu was also on the show, and allowed Gok to have a look at some of her 1960s gear.

Gok exuded in spades was confidence. Indeed, his agent, Carol Hayes, felt that lay behind the secret of his success. 'He always has a solution for every area of his life,' she said. 'He's got a very can-do, don't-worry-about-it attitude and he applies that to his work. So if he's styling a person, it doesn't matter what their problems are in terms of their insecurities; he has the most marvellous way of making it all right.'

She also appreciated his work ethic. 'He has always worked incredibly hard,' she said. 'He will always make sure things are done 150 per cent. He's always done that, even before he was on TV. When he worked as a stylist, people always commented on his energy and commitment. He can't stand letting people down. Privately and as a friend, he is wonderful. It's like having a best friend on tap. I've known him for a long time now and I need only see the look on his face to know what he thinks about what I'm wearing. I can tell when he thinks I've made a boo-boo. But when he says he likes your top, well, it's the best thing in the world.'

One of the side effects of the rise and rise of Gok was that the woman in the street was now looking for more specialist advice. Personal shoppers had always been around, but until now they were seen as part of the high-end of the spectrum, not for just anyone. That was beginning to change. Women like Lorraine Madji, a personal shopper at John Lewis in Edinburgh, were beginning to see their services in demand as never before.

'It may be for a special occasion,' said Lorraine, of the reasons why women sought out her advice. 'Often, we deal with women going back to work after having children. They may have lost their way — you know, become unused to dressing for business. Then you get women who have dressed the same way for 20 years. I can bring them up to date. I don't mean in any high fashion sense but I can suggest a basic capsule wardrobe, a timeless collection of clothes you can take anywhere. Once you have the jacket in a neutral colour, you can match it with almost any colour and have an outfit. A jacket and trousers and smart shirt for daytime can be swapped for a slinky top for the evening. What women don't realise when they come in to John Lewis is that two thirds of the shop floor is of no use to them. It may be the wrong age group, size or colour.'

Lorraine, whose services were free for customers of John Lewis, clearly took her role just as seriously as Gok did his. 'I do my homework,' she said. 'I'll ask them questions about their size and shape, top as well as bottom. I explain to women that their shape changes every few years, as does their colouring. I encourage them to be bold with colour, especially the ones who shop with blinkers on and always avoid a certain colour. I've had divorced women, widowed women, people who have had cosmetic surgery, who all want a new lease of life.'

Again like Gok, some of her work elicted a very emotional response. 'When I've styled them, sometimes they've burst into tears – just because they never realised they could look so fabulous,' said Lorraine. 'I went to see a woman recently and 90 per cent of her wardrobe was black. Well, we ended up giving 80 per cent away to charity. Everything looked exactly the same. Some of the clothes were old, the wrong style and she agreed with me. I make people go through their wardrobe and remove the items they never wear. I tell women not to kid themselves that they will eventually slim into it. I tell them to be ruthless.'

Another Edinburgh-based personal shopper was Annette Lamb, who worked in Harvey Nichols. 'We are always busy, and special times like Christmas are no different from any other,' she said. 'The service is fabulous; I have used it myself in our London shop. It certainly beats trailing round the shops and it's a fun way to spend a few hours doing something different. Having someone take your details then find what you want is better than trying things on which don't fit, having to get dressed, go out and start looking all over again.'

And it wasn't just women who utilised her services. 'The service is more popular with women, but men love personal shopping as well, because they get to sit and watch football on the big screen,' said Annette. 'A lot of men use personal shoppers themselves, but they tend to wait until they really need clothes then spend a lot of money, all in one go. Anybody and everybody is welcome, working women, new mums, business types, footballers. The idea is that people relax yet get their shopping done at the same time.'

The Personal Shopping Manager at the store was Catherine McKenna. 'Customers usually phone first, and by the time they arrive, a number of outfits will have been selected for them to try on,' she said. 'I'm not going to sell something just to make a sale. My job is to help people look their best. I might persuade them to try something new; something a bit different from what they're used to. It doesn't matter if the customer doesn't buy anything, as long as they have a great time. They come in, try on a few outfits, have a meal in the restaurant, have a shower, get their make-up done, dress and go out for the evening.' It was a very Gok-like way to behave.

Gok himself now showed up on *The Charlotte Church Show* and was asked if he, too, would strip naked. Only when the time was right, was the answer. 'I will get naked at some point, but when I do I want a fucking shit load of money for it,' he said. 'I'm saving it. I will save my naked photo for charity and when I'm famous enough, hopefully it will raise millions and that's it – wham, bam, get my knob out!'

He then turned to Katie Price, who was also a guest on the show, and informed her that he used to have a crush on her husband, Peter Andre. 'He was on my bedroom wall when I was 13 and I had so many dirty nights with Peter,' he said. As for Charlotte – she was in a ladette phase. 'Did you ever meet one of the ladies and think, 'What the fuck am I going to do with that?" she asked.

It was a typically outrageous comment, but then Gok was used to raising eyebrows wherever he turned. Asked how to cure a fat day, he replied, 'Have some sex and that is my honest truth. Forget about it for a moment, grab him, get him into bed and then try again afterwards. And do you know what, it doesn't feel as bad.'

*Fashion Fix* continued: next up was the singer Jamelia, who had her own tale to tell about a crisis in a shop. 'My two-year-old spilled a drink over a £20,000 wedding dress I was trying on. But thankfully they didn't make me pay,' she said. 'They Googled me and realised I was famous.'

As the show drew to an end, Gok's advice was still constantly sought after. As autumn 2008 approached, he was asked to give students who would soon be going to university tips on how to dress. His response was to revert to an idea he'd had previously, about most people using clothes in the same way an actor uses a costume. 'The main thing is to understand why we use clothes,' he said. 'It's the easiest way to give people an indication of who we are. When an actor walks on stage, it's the costume that tells you how old they are and what they do. We do this in life, too – it's all to do with identity and image. So when students start university, their outfit on their first day is going to do a lot of work for them.'

The seriousness with which Gok regarded his craft was

evident. Although he was often at pains to stress that he didn't take fashion that seriously, he had clearly put some thought into how people wore clothes and why. And he was right. Changing fashions are a sign of changing societies, to say nothing of presenting a specific idea about one's own personality to the world. Gok himself was always immaculately turned out, sometimes experimenting with a quiff; at others putting a gold streak in his fringe. Stylishness was now a necessity. Gok, too, was judged on his appearance, and given that his world was all about making other people look good, it was imperative that he do the same.

It was at this time, as Gok's popularity was soaring from one peak to the next, that Trinny and Susannah's took a tumble. Ratings figures for *Trinny and Susannah Undress the Nation* were poor: they fell to 2.6 million viewers in the prime-time 9pm slot on ITV1 – just 11.9 per cent of the audience and a world away from the seven million plus figures they had managed with the BBC.

Not that their successors were faring much better: *What Not to Wear*, now hosted by Mica Paris and Lisa Butcher, was being 'rested' by the BBC. The pair were defiant: they posted a message on their website saying, 'The ultimate accolade lies not in viewings ratings or book sales figures, but from the many thousands of letters they receive from women who attest that their confidence, sex appeal and joie de vivre have been restored.'

But that certainly wasn't how everyone else saw it. The

world had moved on and one of the greatest beneficiaries of that was Gok. With his much softer and kinder approach, which was perhaps more necessary in the harsher economic climate in which everyone was beginning to live, Gok seemed to hark back to a gentler world. Many people thought it was simple: Trinny and Susannah were just too cruel. In some quarters they were seen as arrogant. Other celebrities lashed out at them, with Carol Vorderman memorably labelling them as 'an anorexic transvestite and a carthorse in a bin liner.' She was not the only one who felt the girls sometimes went much too far.

That the world was changing was made even more clear when, a couple of days after the viewing figures were released, Gok popped back up on the television screens with a *Naked* two-parter, in which he went back to look at the highlights of the show. The first of the success stories he visited was Lucy Govan, the former tomboy who'd felt fat and unfeminine before Gok took her under his wing. She had now changed utterly from her former self: she had become a plus-sized model and a comedienne.

Another sign of Gok's success was the way his name was now bandied about by people he'd never met, or at least had not worked with him recently. Holly Willoughby, the new presenter on *The X Factor*, was becoming known for her daring, low cut outfits, and revealed that the person behind her look was none other than Simon Cowell. 'He's turned into my stylist, which is a bit weird,' she said. 'Every day he comments on what I'm wearing. He has made comments that I look like a cake and I look like I've been dressed by my mum. He thinks he's Gok Wan.'

It might only have been a passing comment, but it was an indication of the fact that Gok had entered the national consciousness. The meteoric speed of his ascent continued to amaze himself as much as anyone else, but he was up there in the big league. He was one of the major stars of television, courted, wooed and feted, with different channels pursuing him and television production companies keen to find just the right vehicle for him. He was a full-on, undisputed star.

# 12
# EDINBURGH
# NIGHTS

As a major name on television, it was no surprise that Gok made an appearance at the Edinburgh International Television Festival in August 2008. He was interviewed by Nick Higham, who asked him what he made of it all. 'Television people are the worst dressed people in the entire world,' Gok replied. 'I guess it's because they're fun. Creative. They're saying, I don't need to make a big fuss, an example of myself about what I wear, because I'm already very successful.' He was almost certainly right. Gok had spoken a good deal in the past about what clothes said about their wearer, and for rich and successful people to dress down, there was a message there, too.

As usual, Gok was asked about what made *Naked* so successful. 'It's an amazing programme,' said Gok. 'It gives women the opportunity to feel normal, in a good way rather than a bad way. Cuddles, hugs, and being nice to someone. It's watching something good happen.'

But Gok was not at the Festival just to talk about why *Naked* worked so well. He was also participating in an event with senior television executives, in the course of which he managed to get a selection of them to strip down to their undergarments, too. However had he done that? asked Nick Higham.

'I think if you're very gay you can do it,' said Gok. 'It was like a camp cabaret. It was nothing like what you see on TV. There was a lot of flesh, though, more than I thought we were going to get.'

And what of the future? What was Gok going to do next? Something fashion-related, was the answer. 'Fashion is what I love. I don't know what's going to happen,' he declared. 'I never consider myself a television presenter – I'm a fashion stylist who does it on TV.'

Another hot topic was the decline of Trinny and Susannah. Gok could afford to be generous, and he was. 'I feel really sorry for them,' he said. 'There is room for every style of show. All it needs to do is to have a little reinventing. I'm a stylist, not a TV presenter. I work as a stylist and the girls don't. I felt so awkward the other day when I heard the news about their show – I felt so bad for them. This does not spell the end of the make-over show. They are still happening. Everyone wants a good bit of fashion on TV because we all associate with it. But I don't know if Trinny and Susannah can make a comeback. Our shows are completely different and it is too bad that they have bombed.'

But there was a feeling in the air that something had fundamentally changed. The era of the makeover show was far from over, but at the same time, the public wanted something totally different – something they were getting from Gok. Trinny and Susannah's approach, which had worked well when it just came down to advising about clothing, took on a drastically different hue when they were talking to people who had real, deep-rooted problems. It was simply no good barking at people who had been going through a traumatic time.

'I really think Trinny and Susannah ruined it for themselves when they branched out into offering counselling and advice instead of just fashion tips,' said Matt Baylis, the television critic of the *Daily Express*. 'I don't think I've ever come across women who are less sympathetic. They actually give off distaste; you can practically see their nostrils twitching with dislike for someone. It was certainly a step too far for the bulk of viewers.'

The viewers agreed. 'They're posh and patronising, I can't bear to watch any more,' said a former devotee who had switched allegiance to Gok. 'The show actually makes me feel bad because they have such an idealised notion of what you should look like, wear and even achieve in life. I find Gok Wan much more sensitive.'

It was widely agreed that Gok was now much more in keeping with the times. 'Gok Wan has attracted a wider audience, especially with the younger crowd and seems to instil more confidence in his subjects,' said Mark O'Connor, fashion editor of the *Daily Express*. 'Women like to get a male opinion on what to wear and Gok gives them this. Trinny and Susannah have always been about what works with particular figures and not necessarily about solid fashion advice.'

This was very much the experience Gok himself had had. 'I have had women crying in front of me, trying to touch me, telling me how I've changed their lives,' he said. 'It is good-hearted and we try to make a difference. I think the days of nasty TV are over. We don't want to see someone getting slaughtered for wearing the wrong shoes. I don't like this TV dictatorship.' Nor did he like plastic surgery shows. 'They present the options as have plastic surgery and be happy or don't have it and be unhappy.'

There were other issues surrounding all the shows, too. Even Gok was not immune from criticism: after all, he was working in television now, and had to get used to people questioning his motivations. 'I've heard Gok Wan talk about how he used to be "fat and disgusting", but there he is talking to larger women on TV and telling them "big is beautiful",' said Matt Baylis. 'Could this be a little hypocritical? Trinny, 44, and Susannah, 46, say that on the one hand you have to 'accept yourself' but then they try to make people fit into a very definite look. If you were really accepting yourself, it wouldn't matter if you were wearing a grey tracksuit or an evening dress.'

And there were other issues to bear in mind. 'There are the apparent problems, when a job is only half finished or when someone like Julie [on *10 Years Younger*, who had been left in agony after work on her teeth] is left with painful cosmetic dentistry. But there are psychological problems which are just as common, but we hear about them less often,' said one television producer. 'If someone is on a makeover show the chances are all their friends and family will see it, their neighbours, their work colleagues, everyone. If they're made to look an idiot the implications are massive and there's no official procedure for after-care, it's down to the producer's discretion. But producers are under enormous pressure to deliver results and make explosive programmes – even if that means straying quite far from the truth with the end result.'

That was not anything like the case with Gok. However many queries there might have been about his attitude to weight, it was widely accepted that his show set out to do something utterly different from any of the other makeover shows seen on television. And the ratings showed it worked. Women adored him more than ever, and if Gok could get a group of hard-nosed television executives to strip off in front of an audience, he clearly had a touch few other television presenters (even if that was not what he liked to call himself) could call their own.

It was widely felt that Gok's show had an enormous influence in other ways, too. *Gok's Fashion Fix* was very much of the moment, for it was broadcast just as the economy took a sharp turn for the worse, and people began to question the amount they had been spending on clothes. Gok's show was all about making use of high-street stores, and then altering the clothes to achieve an individual look. It was noticeable that across the country, people were beginning to take a much greater interest in sewing their own clothes, and while Gok alone might not have been responsible for that, he had certainly struck a chord.

'Since the beginning of the year, we have noticed a strong trend for customisation,' said Ed Connolly, haberdashery buyer at John Lewis. 'People are realising that old items can be easily updated.'

'Financially it makes a lot of sense, and it's so much greener, too,' said Christa Weil, author of the ethical fashion guide *Heart on Your Sleeve*. 'When shops first started producing these very cute pieces of clothing at enticingly low prices, we all thought, oh yes, but that grab/buy/wear idea is losing its allure.'

Now women were beginning to learn how to sew. Previous generations, with far more of a 'make do and mend' mentality, had been taught by their mothers or at school, but the current generation of young women had none of these traditional skills. So they were going out to learn by themselves. 'Sales of our short courses in sewing skills and garment making have increased by around 28 per cent in the last year,' said Linda Roberts, senior business manager at the London School of Fashion. 'Sewing isn't the only story either — we have added design courses such as Recycled Clothing to appeal to those who want to create a new look from charity shop finds.' Again, this might not all have been because of Gok, but he was certainly attuned to the times.

Given that Gok was now also famous for his enthusiastic championing of every girl's greatest secret, control underwear to perfect the silhouette, it was hardly surprising that he now launched his own range for Simply Yours. However, it was control underwear with a difference. Whereas most underwear designed to hold it in resembled Bridget Jones's big knickers rather than anything a woman might want to show off to a man, Gok's range was designed not only to hold in flesh that needed to be held, but also to look good while it did so. It was an almost certain success right from the outset, but still Gok was nervous about it. This was, after all, a move from styling to designing, quite a different kettle of fish.

'I wanted to make magic underwear that does the trick but which also means that girls can still go home and have sex,' he explained. 'I don't know how many women have said to me over the years that they love wearing magic pants, but they can never let anyone see them with them on. So I wanted to design something that would still give women the confidence they get from control underwear, but in which they would still feel attractive and be able to go home and have sex.'

It was certainly the right field for him. Gok had always talked about the importance of getting the basics right before anything else. 'The first thing I always say to people who I am styling is, "Let's go and have an underwear fitting,"' he said. 'For me, it is so important to get the underwear right. It is the foundation of every single outfit you wear and if you bang on underwear that makes you feel unattractive, it doesn't matter what goes on top. It might be a Christian Dior ball gown or a Chanel jacket, but you are still going to feel unattractive. My ethos for dressing people is that they have got to feel good about themselves. It doesn't matter what you're wearing — you have got to feel confident and that starts with the underwear.'

He had identified a gap in the market: control underwear that actually looked sexy. After that, he looked back to vintage clothing for inspiration. 'Over the years, I have used so many different brands of magic underwear and they all seem to have faults,' he said. 'The biggest of which is the fact that they are generally really, really unflattering. So I decided that I wanted to design control underwear which was sexy and vintage in style. I wanted something which went back to a time when women's bodies were most celebrated and, for me, that was in the Forties and Fifties.'

Fittingly, given Gok's much celebrated love of women, these decades were also a time when women were beginning to take control of their own lives. 'It was post-war, the feminist movement was making an impact and women were suddenly realising that they could do more in life than bring up kids,' he said. 'And, with that, women's clothes really started to change and women began to embrace their bodies. So with my underwear, I wanted to hark back to that era and, for me, it does just that — it looks pin-up and sexy but, most importantly, it does the trick.'

Another difference was that the underwear Gok was

producing catered for a far greater range of sizes than most of the other brands did. Slim women wanted it too, and there was not a lot on offer. Equally, although there was more for the larger lady, there wasn't a great deal of choice. 'I wanted my underwear to cater for as broad a market as possible, so we make from a size eight right up to size 20 and beyond,' he said. 'I know there is not much available for larger girls when it comes to underwear. Both my sister and my mum are larger and often ask me to get them underwear but I just can't because there is so little available. I also know there are slimmer girls who want to use underwear like this as well.'

Nonetheless, it was a nerve-racking time. This was an entirely new venture for him, and Gok wanted to make sure that it worked. 'I have been so nervous about how my underwear will be received,' he said. 'It is such a personal thing and I really want it to work. But, at the same time, I don't want to be seen as one of those TV idiots who pushes themselves on people or just adds their name to something without knowing anything about it. I also didn't want people to feel betrayed by the *How to Look Good Naked* brand either, because I love the show and I know how much it means to the people who watch it. So I was involved in every aspect of creating this underwear, so much so that I think I freaked Simply Yours out a bit.'

He wasn't joking: Gok had been involved with everything from the design process to making sure the material was absolutely right. 'I know just how much effort it took to find fabric that works with the body in a way that it won't ride up or dig in to give women the unsightly lumps and bulges that they can get with other magic underwear,' he said. 'I also know that material allows the skin to breath, that there is so much Lycra in it, it will never lose its shape. It is really durable and, because I know that most women can't afford to spend a lot on underwear, that this stuff will wash really well, too.'

Of course, it was also a fantastic opportunity, and Gok acknowledged as much. Without the success that had come his way, he would never have been given the chance to design his own underwear, and he knew that. Increasingly, it seemed as if the past few years had been almost unreal. 'My life has altered hugely since *How to Look Good Naked* first came on TV,' he said. 'It is a humbling experience, actually. I mean, for the first year all my friends just used to take the piss out of me for being a celebrity, but now I can't imagine my life without the fame.'

But, as Gok realised, it was an unusual position to be in. It's common for television stars to discover that the public thinks they really know them – after all, they're beamed into the centre of the family home – but in Gok's case, it was different. People responded to him in a way they simply didn't with most stars, reacting perhaps to his warmth as well as to the fact he was famous. 'It is a peculiar fame, though, because people feel like they own you, in a way,' said Gok. 'And, in some ways, I suppose they do. What I do on camera is just me. It is not scripted. It is just how I talk and how I gesticulate. So when people see me in the street, they think they know me. I am quite an approachable character, too, so being famous has really affected my life.'

Gok was also delighted by the effect he was having on family life. 'What has been really nice about it all is that mums and daughters are getting together to watch *Naked*, bringing families together again in the sitting room, which is how I was brought up,' he said. 'I also love the fact that we don't really have a strict ABC. Teenagers, gays, straights, men and women all watch the show and that's phenomenal really.'

He had certainly lost none of his charm. He delighted the Irish when, on a visit to Dublin, he protested that their government was not doing enough to promote Irish fashion: 'You've got four million people here – why have we not got more of an Irish stamp? What's going on? I want to talk to your government. You need to be bigging up your fashion scene over here. You need to be promoting big, big, big Irish events, get the people coming in, get the buyers coming in, shipping it all out and get the name out – it's ridiculous.'

The locals loved it, all the more so when Gok was asked if he thought the Irish would look good naked. 'Oh, I fucking bet they can,' he said. 'I'm trying to get a later flight so I can find out. By tomorrow morning I'm planning on getting a little bit of something and I'm not talking about soda bread! I used to have a Dublin boyfriend years ago so we used to take it in turns – I'd come over to Dublin every second weekend. I plan on being mobbed in The George later!' And for the non-gay crowd, he had another message – 'Irish people have got amazing bone structure, I don't know if it's a Gaelic thing,' he said.

And he couldn't resist passing judgment – not all of it flattering – on some of the local celebrities, too. Grainne Seoige was 'too vintage and unsexy', while Blathnaid Ni Chofaigh, hostess on RTE's *The Afternoon Show*, had a 'dull' dress sense. Sheana Keane, also of *The Afternoon Show*, came in for a ticking off, too. 'She needs to get away from that generic TV look,' said Gok. 'She has a really pretty face but she shouldn't hide her body as much. If you've got it, flaunt it.' Nor did the mothers of Dublin, who sometimes took their children to school wearing pyjama bottoms, escape his wrath. 'It's a fucking disgrace,' said an outraged Gok. 'These women need to get their act together and have more pride. They are letting Ireland down.'

But not everyone got it in the neck. Caroline Morahan, formerly the presenter of *Off the Rails*, had been teased a great deal about her daring dress sense. 'People should get off her back,' said Gok. 'She's Ireland's best-looking TV star. She's a cutie and she pushed the boundaries with her dress sense. She's doing something different.'

Caroline herself was rather pleased with his remark, although she pointed out it could have gone either way. 'Isn't it lovely that he said that? That's very nice,' she said. 'But if he's saying something nasty about other people and something nice about me, well, it could just as easily have been the other way around. I sometimes get grief over the way I dress, but it doesn't bother me, not at all.'

Meanwhile, the model Glenda Gilson was definitely doing something right. 'She is hot and sexy,' said Gok. 'Everything about her is right. You can see why she's a top model.' And Lorraine Keane, presenter of *Xpose*, was also doing well: 'She knows how to pose and she's got great legs,' said Gok. 'She should show those babies off all the time.' Rosanna Davison, a former Miss World, came in for mixed praise.: Gok called her 'a complete hottie' but added, 'She gets it really right or really wrong – there's no middle ground. But I like that.'

Gok was actually in Dublin for a serious reason: he had been made the head of a campaign to make glasses cool, and he was there to award the prize of Irish Spectacle Wearer of the Year to Limerick girl Nicola Bennett. The 22 year-old won an Assets modelling contract and went on to the finals of Specsavers Spectacle Wearer of the Year. School children were bullied for wearing glasses (as Gok had been) and he was doing what he could to help future generations. 'Classroom taunts can cause long-term damage to a child's self-esteem and their education,' he said. 'It's difficult to believe that children are still being called names for wearing glasses, especially considering many celebrities are regularly photographed wearing the latest geek-chic styles. I want children to know they are not abnormal, they are not freaks, they are just kids who happen to wear glasses.'

Michelle Elliot, the founder of Kidscape, agreed. 'Bullies are cowards who look for some reason to pick on kids and often use glasses as an excuse,' she said. 'We want to give some confidence back to these kids and show them they are not different or geeky, they are actually really cool.'

Meanwhile, the search was on for the next project that would be right for Gok. It was decided it would be a series called *Gok's Beauty Show*, and an advertisement was duly placed, calling on the women of Britain to sign up:

## CALLING ALL FABULOUS FEMALES!
## GOK WAN WANTS YOU.

So are you proud of what you look like and who you are? Do you think you could be Great Britain's most beautiful hot babe or if not maybe you, someone you know like a friend or family member?

Gok Wan guru of style is launching a Great British search. Curvy, slender, natural or glam, tiny to tall, unconventional beauty or cat walk model material... He wants you all for his brand new series.

Gok's new show is all about beauty that's more than just skin-deep. Full of great challenges, big surprises, packed with top tips and glamorous bits — it's the show every gorgeous gal should be part of. Don't miss out!

However, it was not just a beauty show: it was to be about all aspects of the beauty industry, including products, treatments and what could sometimes go wrong.

It was not often that Gok was savaged in the press (apart from male TV critics), but for some reason the announcement of that show seemed to needle the writer

Julie Burchill, who wrote a piece warning women that Gok was not their gay best friend. 'Mr Wan has successfully seen off the two-headed atrocity that was Trinny and Susannah with his Channel 4 show, *How to Look Good Naked*; wow, dig the logic there!' she wrote. 'A man who is, by definition, at best unmoved and at worst repelled by the naked female form being paid to show you sad bitches how not to make men run screaming for the sanctuary of the gay bar.'

Gok, going from strength to strength, appeared unmoved by her tirade. He could afford to be. He was more in demand than ever, although there was a downside in that he didn't see his family as much as he once did. 'For a long time I was my parents' son and now they have to share me with the world,' said Gok, a touch melodramatically. 'I also work so much now, it limits the time I can see them. It's tough but we've worked out ways of dealing with it. I feel out of sorts if I don't speak to my mum regularly. If I was starry, I might get more time off work, but unfortunately, I've spent so may years working behind the camera that I have that crew mentality and I graft too much. But I always think, "You're only as good as your last job."'

Increased fame had caused other problems, too. In the past, Gok had spoken a great deal about the journey he made with the women he styled, and the bond that went on to exist between the two, but these days there were so many women that these bonds simply couldn't all be maintained. And, not surprisingly given the way he managed to boost their egos, the women could become a little clingy. Gok represented hope and the future for them, and some clearly didn't want to let go. For Gok, however, this was not so welcome, so he had to disengage gently.

'They do stay in touch, but I have to cut them short a little bit because they become quite dependent,' he said. 'In the beginning, when it was a new show, I exchanged phone numbers and I didn't know what the effect was going to be. It was a bit of a mistake. Now I don't. It's not that I don't care – it's just not really fair on either of us. If they have a down day, they have nowhere to turn, so they automatically come to me and I feel the responsibility. But it's probably best for them to stand on their own two feet.'

It was the price of fame: everyone wanted a piece of Gok now. However, doing the shows took their toll as well. Gok confessed that he sometimes felt so wrung out at the end of it all, that he too required professional help. 'When you're filming a show like this and you're dealing with women who hate their bodies, you need somewhere to let it all out,' he said. 'I'm not a doctor or a psychologist, but I have to take it on as their friend, and I realised I was feeling quite stressed out with it. If you can imagine eight of your best girlfriends, all of them going through the most horrific time and needing you, and only you, it's a lot to take on board. You become a sponge. Of course I do take it on because I care for them, but I need to get rid of it as well. But once I've let it out, it's gone. As soon as I stop filming, I stop seeing my counsellor.'

Success in romance, however, continued to elude him. Gok might have been the highest-profile gay man on television, but since splitting from the partner he had never named, he had not managed to find a replacement friend. Still, he was philosophical about it. 'I haven't got time for much at the moment, but I'm auditioning for a boyfriend,' he told one interviewer. 'I'll always be auditioning – I'm like an old Broadway play. My ideal partner? Do you know what? I think the reason why I'm still auditioning is that I don't know. I've got no clue. I'm hoping that one day my Prince Charming will just arrive on a huge stallion and then he'll show me exactly what I've been looking for. I've got no complaints about my life. I've got great family, friends and an amazing job – two shows on the go – and if anything else comes along, it's a bonus.'

But underneath, he was still the same old Gok. He might have become a little more cautious towards the women he worked with, and he knew now that it was difficult for him to go out without being mobbed, but essentially, he was still himself. Indeed, he even maintained that he sometimes needed advice on his appearance, too. 'Of course! I ask everyone,' he said. 'My flatmate gets it in the neck every single day. Every time I go out, I'm thinking, "What shall I wear?" Unfortunately for her, I have a lot of clothes, so it takes a lot of time before I find the right outfit.'

He was also as good natured as ever, and conceded that years of working as a stylist to the stars, and having to remain tactful with it, might well have been why he was so good with ordinary women today. 'All the celebs I have worked with have been absolutely amazing, and I love them all dearly,' he said. 'At the end of the say, I still have to work as a stylist, so I have to be as tactful as possible. So many people do feel bad about their bodies. I come along and say, "Actually, you don't need to change. You don't have to look a certain way – just work with what you've got." I like to think I'm a nice person and I'd never hurt any of the women I work with. I would never tell a woman she looked horrible, but I would tell her she looked fabulous.'

It was the secret of his success and it showed no signs of waning. Gok loved what he did and it showed: he also had a natural empathy with his subjects and a strong enough personality to stand out on screen. On one hand, he was every woman's gay best friend; on the other a sparkling television personality, who held his own with the best of them. The world, and all it held, was at his feet.

# 13
# THE SUPERSTAR
# NEXT DOOR

One of the reasons for Gok's success, it was widely agreed, was his great empathy with women. But another was that despite the fact that his height, weight, racial background and sexual orientation had set him apart at school, at the same time there was something endearingly boy-next-doorish about him. Had he been interested in women, any mother would have been delighted to have him as a son-in-law. And despite his huge success, he still admitted to the same doubts and insecurities as everyone else. He may have lost the excess weight some years previously, but he still knew what it was like to feel worried about yourself.

'The reason I can empathise with women so much is because I realise how they feel about their bodies,' he said. 'I've got certain tricks I do with mine to make me feel better about myself, that I try to teach to women. But I work at it every day like everyone else and whenever someone comes on to *Naked*, I say to them, "You're not going to feel so confident about your body that you won't have any hang-ups at the end, and it's not going to happen overnight, either. But it will give a different personal perception about how other people view your body. I've had to do the same thing for myself."'

But it had worked. Gok had come to terms with what he looked like — very much so — and he had lost many of the hang-ups he'd had in the past. 'I love full-length mirrors!' he said. 'Clothes are really important to me, and so when I look in the mirror, I'm loving my outfit! I don't think I'll ever be 100 per cent happy with my body, but I've taught myself ways of dealing with that. It doesn't stop me having intimate relations with people — I love sex! It's not going to stop me buying clothes. It's not going to stop me going on holiday.'

Indeed, Gok appeared to be moving from being a style consultant to a complete lifestyle guru. He oozed optimism and positivity. He had turned his life around, was the message, and now other people could do so, too. It was not simply the case that he was a kind man, encouraging women to see their bodies in a better light: he was telling people that with a positive attitude, they could do almost anything. It was an immensely encouraging message, and entirely in keeping with how Gok ran the rest of his life.

'I don't want to be miserable any more. I want to enjoy myself, and I'm scared that I'm going to lose it all tomorrow,' he said, referring to his lust for life, not material gain. 'I'm actually petrified that I'll drop down dead tomorrow... What, miss out on this? I'm having the best time. I say to women, "Well, I've done it – the proof's in the pudding." It can be done. You too can have a fantastic life.'

Meanwhile, the rest of the world continued to sing his praise. Carol Vorderman, who had had a very public spat with Trinny and Susannah, was one of them. 'My real heroes are people like astronauts and scientists,' she said. 'But I've been watching Gok Wan and really love what he does. Do I feel good naked? Yes – but I won't inflict it on the public.' Not for the first time, Carol Voderman spoke for the public: as a kind of glamorous girl-next-door, she quite frequently found herself able to give voice to the public mood, and she had certainly done so now.

She wasn't the only one to love Gok. A survey of more than 1,000 people on their way to *TNT* magazine's Winter Travel Show showed that he would be most women's ideal holiday companion. That produced derision from some quarters ('a nookie free fortnight, then, ladies,' wrote one wag) but it would have been of no surprise to anyone following his career. Gok made women feel happy about themselves. Not only that, but he was fun, exciting, glamorous, with energy, charm and enthusiasm. Merely to be in his presence was a cheering experience, especially for people who had for so long struggled with issues of self-esteem. What wasn't to like?

Alan Carr, with whom Gok had appeared on *The Friday Night Project*, was another fan. 'Yeah. He was brilliant,' he said. 'I saw in him a lot of me as well. I think he's very sensitive. I think we should do a remake of that horror movie together, *Whatever Happened to Baby Jane?*' Indeed, the two were becoming matey behind the scenes: when Alan interviewed Gok for *More* magazine, Gok told him: 'I know your boyfriend really well. I used to date him.' The two of them egged one another on: while sometimes there seemed to be competition in the campness stakes, at others the two of them resembled nothing so much as naughty schoolboys, out to shock.

But he wasn't always a saint. In the autumn of 2008, Victoria Beckham chose to unveil her latest look: a pixie crop that took years off her. Gok was not impressed. 'It kind of looks as if you imagine you're going into the back of the Royal Palladium on a Saturday night, and it's the big gig, and Shirley Bassey's getting ready to go on stage. And she runs out there without enough time to put her wig on. I'm kind of getting that feeling from it, I'm going to be honest, as if she's forgotten something.'

Then he relented. 'I'm a bit of a Victoria fan,' he went on. 'I feel very sorry for them because they are just completely under the microscope. We all talk about them constantly.' Everyone talked about Gok pretty constantly too, these days: he knew what it was like to live in the spotlight. He also knew that he just had to open his mouth these days, and it made the news.

His influence continued to be felt, too. The television presenter Dawn Porter was back with a new series exploring all things female, and the first programme was called 'Dawn Gets Naked': it was hard to miss Gok's influence there. (For the record, Dawn did her bit, taking part in a burlesque show and organising a naked flash mob in central London.) Everyone seemed to be clamouring to do something with naked in the title, to say nothing of stripping off when the occasion demanded – had not Trinny and Susannah done exactly that? Ironically enough, the exception was Gok. He continued to tease, promising a naked shot one day, but for now at least he was covering up.

Another element of the Gok effect was that he had brought the role of a stylist to the wider domain. Trinny and Susannah were not stylists as such: they were two women who had a good instinct for which clothes suited a person and had used this, until recently, to very successful effect. Gok, on the other hand, was a stylist, and his approach differed from theirs in far more than just the tone of voice he used.

As well as being a champion of the high street, Gok was passionately interested in high fashion, the kind of experimental approach that could result in quite spectacular looks. Stylists like him could be hugely important in the world of fashion. Carine Roitfeld, for example, the editor of French *Vogue* and one of the best dressed women in the world, had worked as a stylist for years before taking on editorial leadership of the magazine. This was the field in which Gok worked.

Of course, he also embraced the high street, not least because the subjects on his show could not afford to deck themselves out head to toe in Dior, but on top of this he was teaching people how to make the high street work for them. In *Gok's Fashion Fix* he even took on the big names with his own high-street styled outfits, but even so, his background was in the most fashion-forward section of the industry and he had not forgotten whence he came.

Indeed Gok had now become so popular that he was doing a Celebrity Master Class at the Fashion Retail Academy, something that must have been a first. Master classes are usually held for musicians, actors or dancers, not stylists or people who work in the fashion world. But Gok was changing that. 'Basically, I'm giving some kids an insight into what I do,' he explained. 'It'll cover the full process of a styling job, from consultation and research through to the actual buying, as well as the styling and the presentation of the clothes. A whole styling job in a day with 21 young people watching me: it's going to be a cracker!'

And, of course, he was as much in demand for style advice as ever. 'There are three big looks I'm loving,' he said of the trends emerging in autumn 2008. 'Heritage is all about old English style and dressing, the kind of thing you would expect the Queen to wear out hunting. It's tweeds and plaids and has got a real, old British feel. Another one is Highland, which is tartan themes; tartan is just one of my favourite prints ever! Very regal, actually. You know what? We are going back to a more suitable way of dressing. My nan would prefer it to some of the styles that have been around for the last few years!

'However, as well as these more traditional styles we have got this huge gothic rock trend – beautiful, elegant, heavily embellished. It's a bit Munsters, but I do like it! So those three trends are all about heavy prints, lots of tweeds, lots of layering and slightly more costume. We are definitely getting more adventurous, and it's about time!'

The time Gok was talking about was a time in which the economic climate had begun to take a turn for the worse. It has always been known that there's a link between fashion and the economy, and in what he was describing, Gok was actually talking about a return to a very traditional look at a time when everyone was beginning to feel increasingly insecure. Could the two have been linked? Even for those who were not directly affected by the economic downturn, a feeling seemed to be growing that the nation had indulged in too much excess.

Tweeds, twin sets and regal looks harked back to a more austere age, one in which it was not the done thing to 'max out' the credit card. Equally, however, the more luxurious look Gok was describing might also have been in response to the times. When times are tough, it can be reassuring to glam up. Either way, he was describing a new feeling in the air that was not just tied to how people looked.

For all that, people were still shopping, and Gok also felt that the actual process of buying clothes had changed. 'Fashion has become more accessible,' he said. 'The process from catwalk to high street takes about nine weeks now, so we're much more trend-savvy and we have so many different styles going on. Whether you want the indie look or the emo look, there is so much choice and a bigger market. That's why there is a need for more people to work in the industry.' He was certainly doing his bit for the cause.

But if that was the case, he was asked, then why was retail sometimes seen as an alternative to a real job? 'I don't know,' Gok admitted. 'It's changing though: we have a slightly more American set-up now with glamorous, high-profile fashion roles such as buyers and merchandisers. When you're buying for a high-street retailer you have a lot of creative control, because you are deciding whose brands to stock. More and more people are aware of what it is to be a buyer or a merchandiser; the prestige gives people another reason to get involved. Unfortunately, there is still a taboo in this country about working in a shop. We need to start respecting the industry more than we do currently.'

Unsurprisingly, the retailers of Britain loved him for that. But then he really did have a habit of lifting the mood of the people around him, as evidenced by the reaction when he visited the Simply Yours offices. The company manufactured his lingerie range, and his visit showed that, successful though he might be, a diva he most certainly was not. Some celebrities can be very aloof when meeting people they consider to be less important than themselves: where Gok was concerned, nothing could have been further from the truth. He made quite as much effort with them as he ever had done with anyone on his show, and the girls present were thrilled to meet him, and posted their experiences on a colleague's blog.

'I was absolutely mortified when Gok Wan came into the office calling out my name, but he came over and gave me a big hug, which immediately put me at ease,' wrote Sam, one of the women involved. 'Gok said I had a "great 1950s thing going on" but I needed more support for my boobs and something to accentuate my waist. So I went and tried on pieces from the Gok Wan lingerie range, settling on the Banger Booster bra and the Super Slicker Knickers.' The names of the pieces, incidentally, were classic Gok, combining humour with practicality while ladling on some glamour.

The girls loved them. 'The Gok knickers were a lot more comfortable than I expected and gave me a really smooth silhouette without holding me in too much,' wrote Sam. 'Other shapewear I've tried is too tight on the tummy and gives me tummy ache. The Banger Booster supported my boobs and gave me a great cleavage. I love how you can adjust the bra straps to cross over at the back. I've got very narrow shoulders and this makes me feel really secure.'

Above all, though, Gok put Sam at her ease. He made a fuss of her, as he had done with so many women, boosted her confidence and made her feel comfortable with herself. It was the Gok effect in action again: this quite extraordinary ability to get anyone to relax. 'Gok was lovely – very funny and caring and made me feel special,' she continued. 'So special that I was happy to stand in front of him and a film crew in just my bra and knickers!'

Another of the girls involved was Sophie, and she was

just as won over by his charm as everyone else. 'Gok is really nice, very friendly and reassuring,' she said. 'Although he did make a holy show of me by pulling my knickers up out the back of my skirt whilst I was stood at my desk! The underwear felt really nice on and made a big difference to stomach and my waist! I wore the Curve Controller body shaper and it felt very nice and quite sexy on (although I did have to put my heels on too).'

Fortuitously, it was Gok's birthday, so the girls were able to make a fuss of him, too. 'You could tell he was very genuine when he gave us compliments and kept telling us how fabulous we looked!' said Sophie. 'We sang happy birthday to him and had some cake. Gok was lovely and I would definitely recommend the Gok Wan underwear to ladies of all shapes and sizes, because it not only does it job but it makes you feel very slinky!'

Finally there was Michelle. 'Well, where do I start – apart from Gok stating I had great bangers!' she said. 'Until I tried on the Gok Wan lingerie I didn't believe that my assets could actually be lifted – I thought that they would permanently stay south! I was fitted into a Gok bra, waist control pants and the boned corset [and] all I can say on behalf of the larger lady – wow!'

Michelle was a typical example of someone whose self image went through the roof after a chat with Gok. She also couldn't quite believe how he had made her look. 'I actually had a figure: my waist came back which I had not seen for the last 19 years and to be honest I was amazed at the results,' she said. 'I do not really dress up underneath my clothing but I have now had the Gok Wan lingerie for a week and can now safely say that I would buy most of the products – they make you feel really good about yourself.'

Gok himself was enormously proud of the range. It was, 'inspired by the support-wear of the 1940s and 1950s, that whole pin-up thing, when women actually had a bit of flesh on them but, rather than dieting and exercising, they employed a bit of structural engineering,' he said. 'I am very hands on, and I am always saying to women, "How does it fit?" because of course I'm not going to wear it, that's the problem.' Except that he did. In order to find out what it felt like to spend your time in control underwear, Gok had spent a week wearing it himself. It was not a pleasant experience, although it did give him a valuable insight into what women had to go through to look good.

'They crucified me,' he said of the big pants. 'They rode up and down and you could see them over my jeans. What I wanted to do was develop something that stayed invisible and allowed you to move but when you took your clothes off, still looked incredibly sexy.' His range of lingerie has since been a great success: he had clearly identified a market that no one had yet entirely been able to take on board.

As well as branching out into lingerie, Gok was still going from strength to strength on television. The next project was to be the show for which girls had been invited to enter a beauty competition. It had a name now, *Miss Naked Beauty*, and it certainly wasn't going to be a conventional beauty contest. The girls were to be set a series of challenges, including being photographed without make-up or any of the props they'd brought with them. These women were different from the *Naked* women in that they didn't appear to have the same degree of self-loathing, but they were called upon to do a great deal more than simply sit around and look pretty.

'The show will turn the traditional beauty contest on its head with the winner being all about raw natural beauty, but also having brains and balls,' said a source close to the show. 'A total of 10,000 women have already applied, with the first show whittling them down to just 12. They will battle it out for the title of Channel 4's beauty ambassador.'

There was also a good deal of speculation about how Gok and his new co-host Myleene Klass would come across together on screen. 'It's going to be a funny partnership – Myleene is the girl for whom butter wouldn't melt in her mouth, while Gok is never one to keep his thoughts to himself. We'd like to see Gok try to get Myleene to strip off – she might wallop him!'

Like Alexa before her, Myleene was an inspired choice to pair with Gok. A classically trained musician, she eventually found fame with the pop group Hear'Say after appearing on *Popstars*. Subsequently she'd had a great deal of television presenting experience, along with a very successful appearance on *I'm A Celebrity…* Her appearance in a swimsuit rocketed her profile sky high, leading to a modeling contract with Marks & Spencer, but above all it was her sparky personality that won people round. Lively and opinionated, popular with men but also very much a girls' girl, Myleene's appearance was bound to provide more attention to the show.

But it was Gok's gig above all, and he adopted the same approach towards these new charges that he had done in the past. Increasingly it was clear that his experience with the many celebrities he'd styled, and the need for tact, had been invaluable in preparing him for his current role. 'I don't walk into a job and say, "Listen, love, you're on the TV, you're in the films but you're too fat, you need to go on a diet, I'll see you in two weeks' time,"' he said. 'Instead I say, "Right, you're perfect. Let's get you a few dresses and let's get you some good underwear and let's get you on that red carpet feeling good about yourself, because your pictures are going to be beamed around the world!"'

Nor would he berate them about weight. 'I would never, that's not my job to say that, that's absolutely not my position to say that at all,' said Gok adamantly. 'If someone had said that to me when I was 21 stone, I would have sat on them. Absolutely, that isn't my role to do that, I'm not a doctor, I'm not a dietician.' Nor did he hector or prescribe: his mantra remained the same. Love yourself and work with what you've got. It worked with celebrities and it worked with the woman on the street.

Gok also maintained that he was totally non-judgmental about the way people dressed, even if he was not a personal fan of their style. 'Fashion is about costume and identity, it's about being who you are, and you've got to have a certain amount of confidence to be in the public eye to be able to do it,' he said. 'So when I look at people for what they're wearing, I might not like it but I understand that fashion and image is so subjective, it's not down to my opinion. It's about confidence. It's about understanding your identity, and why you do certain things, and so I respect all people for what they wear. I might not like it, but that's more of a taste thing.'

But it was no longer a case of whether or not Gok was nice to people: he was on the receiving end as well. Being a public figure carries with it many blessings, but it does open you up to attack, and Gok had experienced that, too. It had made him more wary. Nor had he found the experience of very sudden fame easy to deal with. 'It was awful,' he said. 'There's a fat kid inside me that still wants to be liked. I'm not a horrible person, I hope people see that. I have a big heart and I'm not perfect and I probably swear too much and drink too much Stella and I'm too opinionated … but I've had some horrible stuff written about me and it kills me, absolutely destroys me.'

Although he wasn't explicit, that would seem to refer to his unfortunate experience with Daisy Idwal Jones. Gok had never publicly responded to her accusations, other than to say he'd been devastated by them, but it was clearly an experience that ran deep. Indeed, given the extent of his popularity, in many ways it was a surprise he was quite as fearful of bad publicity as seemed to be the case. Put simply, compared to most people, he got remarkably little negative coverage. People still loved him: in a lot of female eyes, Gok really could do no wrong.

And it was increasingly evident that his show had done a lot of real good. Gok had been back to see some of the women he'd worked with and they'd been transformed. 'I've just done six revisits and I was thinking, "If I turn up after all this hard work and it hasn't been amazing, where do I stand then? Is it not real?"' he said. 'There was one woman, Lucy, she hated her body, she was working on a farm – and now she's a model and a stand-up comedian!

'There's a woman who's had another baby – she'd not had sex for years. And there was Helen – big boobs, fabulous girl, who was living in Scunthorpe, miserable, had two children – who said to her husband after the show, "You dragged me up here to do your job – I want a career again, I'm strong..." She now runs her own business and flies all over the place. Every one of them has achieved so much and I'm so made up about that – it's phenomenal.' And it was all down to him. He hadn't just made these women look good: he'd restored their confidence in themselves, possibly the most valuable gift of all.

Gok was particularly proud of one subject. Asked about his biggest transformation, he replied, 'Probably Kelly, who was the last show of series four of *How to Look Good Naked*. She'd had a mastectomy. It was really hardcore, tough work – a lot of issues – but amazing. It was a challenge for me because I wasn't doing the usual simple, low-level body dysmorphia. It was a different kind of body-loathing, and she was so soon out of surgery as well, so we went on a personal journey together. I think that was the biggest transformation, the one that sticks in my memory.'

The critics might have carped, but undeniably something was going on. Gok himself professed to be startled by the full realisation of what he had achieved. 'I didn't know I could change someone's life. I was probably the most sceptical out of everyone when we started,' he said. 'Doing *Naked* was an eye-opener as I never knew how bad it had got. I knew that some women didn't like their bodies, but I didn't realise that 98 per cent of women hate their bodies, I was blown away. I think women have been pressurised for so long to look a certain way it is out of control – there is this massive cloud of doom hanging over most women's bodies.'

And for the women who came on to *Naked*, their self loathing was such that it was ruining their lives in some cases. 'Every one of them feels pressurised to look a certain way, and as they don't look that way they feel they can't be successful, or happy, or loved – all the nice stuff in life has been taken away from them,' Gok said. But he was helping to restore it, to rebuild these fragile women, and he clearly loved what he did.

At the end of the show the women had voluntarily undressed. Gok was adamant that there was no pressure on them whatsoever to do so: they were ready to show the world that their relationships with their bodies had changed. 'You know what, if it was just for TV, I wouldn't do it as I'm the biggest arsehole on that programme. I'm screaming and shouting at the channel and the execs constantly, no one could force me to impose that on women,' he said. It was a slightly different side to him from the one the public was used to, but then Gok did come from a family that frequently got carried away when it came to arguments. He had his high-maintenance side, but he was careful only to use it on those who could fight back.

He did, however, concede that occasionally it had been a bit touch and go when it came to getting the women to parade their all. 'It's been close on a few occasions,' he said. 'But the naked thing is really important to me because I want to turn around to all these women and say, "You know what, babe, your husband hasn't seen you naked for ten years, you've not had sex for 20 years, your life is being dictated by how you feel about your body. I'm going to make you realise how absolutely beautiful you are and that you have a right on this earth to stand there and be proud of who you are."'

Nor had he ever met a woman he couldn't help. 'I never look at anyone and go, "No". I look at people and think, "Challenge! Let me at 'em, let me have a go!"' he said. 'I think it comes from my own personal experiences of body-loathing. And I understand clothes. I get clothes. Not everyone does, and it's quite fortunate that I do, otherwise I'd be out of a job! When I look at someone and think, "Right, you need help," it allows me to show off a little bit, and think, I can do this.'

At the bottom of it all, however, remained the great irony. Gok, this marvellous saviour to women, was gay. He might have made the women feel wonderful about themselves, teach them how to look good both naked and with clothes on and repair their damaged self-esteem, but he couldn't give them what most women really want from a man — making love. Nor could they give it to him. Gok spent his life surrounded by women, but his real interests, as he had always made abundantly clear, lay elsewhere. So could Gok take that final step? Could he weave his magic on men?

# 14

# HOW TO LOOK GOOD NAKED – FOR MEN

So there it was: possibly the most famous gay man on television had never worked with men. Women adored him (and fancied him), but Gok's natural constituency, as it were, was still a closed book. But why not explore it? In these image-obsessed times, men were almost as worried about their appearance as women, so why not let Gok loose on a few male subjects for a change?

Gok had previously ruled it out of the question, but he was beginning to have a rethink. Indeed, he had completely changed his mind. He'd been doing the show for a while now, and had worked with people in very difficult situations, which meant his own confidence was greater than it had been previously. So why not?

'Yeah, I want to do it. Really 100 per cent,' said Gok, when tackled on the subject. 'When they first asked me if I would, I said no, absolutely not, because I didn't feel confident enough with what I was doing. And I did the show with Kelly and it gave me a completely different confidence in what I did. I thought, you know what? I've done it now with a woman who's been through a huge, huge, massive struggle in her life, and as much as she took all the stuff away from the show, I took away a lot away from her show as well, and I thought, I'm going to give it a go. So next series, I'm going to get guys on the show.'

This really would be an innovative step. Gok was not the first to front a makeover show and men had appeared on some of these programmes, most notably Trinny and Susannah's, but there had never been a programme that really was devoted to male subjects. Nor was the help and support elsewhere available to men in the way that it was to women, and Gok was aware of that, too. 'I think men have it really hard as well but they don't have a social vehicle or a voice,' he said. 'They have bloody *Men's Health* – I think my brother buys it because he's a bodybuilder – and that's about it.'

He was right. Yet at the same time, it was known that men, too, were turning to plastic surgery (albeit in not quite such numbers as women), and the pressure was there to look young, too. Terms such as 'metrosexual', to describe such highly groomed individuals as David Beckham, were becoming commonplace. Men were beginning to wear cosmetics and make-up, so why not teach them how to dress properly, too?

Of course, there were risks. Gok's notoriously tactile approach was all very well when it came to women, but men? Would they feel comfortable being pawed about by another man, especially a gay one? Nor had he always been particularly complimentary about straight men. 'Straight guys bore me a bit,' he once confessed. 'They haven't got much personality, have they? If I meet a new straight guy he either wants to out-gay me, or he spends hours trying to explain how fine he is with my sexuality.'

Men also tended to be more proud than women, less in touch with their feelings and not necessarily happy to own up to major self-loathing. So it was quite a gamble, but it was one Gok was prepared to take. Although he couldn't resist throwing in the odd joke, not least on the subject of Simon Cowell. 'I've got a real soft spot for Simon,' he said. 'The only challenge would be his trousers – how quickly I could get them off.'

Men weren't taking up a great deal of Gok's personal life, either. Although he was always happy to joke about auditioning for a boyfriend, in actual fact his fame was making it more difficult for him to find a new relationship than you would have thought. Viewers had preconceptions about him, men and women alike, and that caused problems when he met someone new. 'People see me as Gok the homo from TV and it's a massive barrier because people don't get through that,' said Gok rather sadly, and it was true: he had become a commodity to be beamed into people's sitting rooms.

People he had never met felt they knew him. It didn't make it easy to find the right person and, just as high-profile women have sometimes found it difficult to find a man content to live in their shadow, so the same applied to a gay man. Anyone who became Gok's partner was going to have to be prepared to be subjected to a great deal of scrutiny, which was more than a great many men would be willing to take.

Nor was Gok's workload a help. He was enormously busy these days and as he pointed out, had no time for romance. 'I'm too busy to have a shower, let alone find a chap,' he said. 'I had a huge crush on Tony Blair, in a totally sexual way. He was so powerful but nerdy at the same time. That's so my ideal man – a bit geeky but strong.' But while Gok was teasing, there was a note of sadness behind it all. What, after all, is success, if there is no one to share it with?

In light of all that, it was ironic that a poll came out in October 2008, naming Gok as women's number one dream date. More than that: he was also the one most would consider leaving their husbands for. Gok took it in his stride: 'They wouldn't have much of a sex life, but they'd look damn good,' he said.

This poll certainly said something, though. It was indicative not only of Gok's effect on women, but what women really wanted from a man. Some of these women might have been deluding themselves that if only they could get their hands on Gok, they could make a straight man of him yet, but the vast majority knew he was gay and thus very unlikely to wish to sleep with them — and yet they didn't care.

Gok offered warmth and sympathy, someone to chat to, who didn't judge and didn't make unpleasant remarks. 'Whether it's feeling good about your body, or getting designer looks on a high street budget, I'm all about making people feel better about themselves,' he said. 'People feel safe around me because they know I'm not going to bullshit them or back them into a corner to get TV results.' In every way apart from his sexuality, he was the perfect man for most women. The irony was lost on no one, not least on Gok himself.

At least business was going well. His lingerie range, which Gok described as 'gripper knickers with bows on', was continuing to sell very well. Gok was in a challenging mood about it all. 'I don't shy away from the word fatty at all,' he said. 'I think it's a perfectly fine term. But my range is for everybody. Magic underwear is not about whipping everything away, it's about getting your bits back into proportion. If you're a size eight, you can still be a pear shape with saggy tits. Even Kate Moss would look great in my Sassy Slip.' In fact Kate Moss would look great in anything, but the point about Gok's range of lingerie was that it was designed to make all women feel as though they looked like Kate Moss.

Gok was also rather proud of the fact that he'd tried it out on himself. 'I knew some people would say: "How can a gay man, who clearly doesn't wear that kind of underwear, be making it for women?" So I spent a month trying it out,' he said. Did he try his Banger Booster bra, one interviewer asked. 'Don't be silly,' said Gok. 'Do I look as though I need to boost my bangers? I tried out the corsets and the shorts. I wanted to know how they felt. But I have to admit, I looked fucking hideous in a sex-kitten corset.'

Women, however, looked very nice in them. 'It looks incredibly sexy,' said Gok. 'It's all designed from the Forties and Fifties. It gives you the support that you need but when you go to get that shag, you're still going to look good when you take your clothes off instead of looking like an artificial limb in beige spandex.'

With all this talk of bringing men on to the show, Gok began to think about designing support underwear for them, too. 'Guys don't have the right vocal or social platform to talk about body loathing,' he said. 'Why shouldn't men have magic underwear? Guys are constantly moaning about their moobs. Maybe I could design a man bra and get Simon Cowell to market it for me.' If anyone were to design such a range, Gok was clearly the man to do it, but it would be quite a feat to pull off, even for him.

Indeed, everything was going so well that Gok was able to express sympathy for Trinny and Susannah. 'They've had it taken away from them and they're clearly going through a rough patch,' he said. 'We just do things very differently. I'm a working stylist, they're from PR backgrounds. And I'm not a misogynist. I have to empower my clients.'

Gok couldn't resist the odd moment of cattiness, however,

when asked what he thought of the appearance sported by some celebs. Victoria Beckham, in particular, came in for some stick. 'Posh never gets it wrong — or right,' he said. 'She's like the Habitat of fashion. She doesn't do anything wrong, but she doesn't get anything particularly right, either. I just don't get her. It's uncreative and uninventive. Fashion should be fun but Victoria's never playful.'

Chaka Khan, on the other hand, was something else. 'It'd be a big job but I'd love to style her,' said Gok. 'I love Chaka Khan — she's a ball of fire. But she dresses so badly. She's asked me to style her but I haven't had time yet. She's a big body with a big booty and bangers. And big mental hair. I'd like to get my hands on her. That would be a big job.'

Another person Gok would have liked to style was Jordan. 'I'd love to strip off all of Jordan's make-up and start again,' he said. 'She's stunning and I'd do something very classic with her. She'd look absolutely great in early 1970s, Sophia Loren-style clothes.'

Anyone who dismissed this as just playful bitchery underestimated Gok's very real influence on the fashion world. By October 2008, economic slowdown was well on the way, yet the catalogue retailer N Brown revealed that half-year pre-tax profits had risen 20 per cent to £40.8 million. One of the reasons for this was that its customers tended to be older and own their own homes, which meant they were less likely to be affected, but another reason was their new ranges, including one by Gok. When your influence is such that it helps buck economic trends when it comes to retail spending, you are truly a person with power in the fashion world.

Gok continued to be on demand on television, appearing with Dawn French on *Al Murray's Happy Hour*. His charm showed through in everything he did: the latest woman to experience the Gok Wan brand of charm was Nicola O'Donnell, who had won £250 worth of Dorothy Perkins clothing vouchers and a session with Gok. She seemed almost as thrilled with that latter as she was with the clothes.

'I hadn't really read the competition details properly and thought I was entering to win £250 of clothes which, in itself, would have been great,' said Nicola, a mother-of-three, who had recently lost a good deal of weight and was now trying to work out what sort of clothes to wear. 'But when I was told I had won the clothes and a meeting with Gok Wan, that was even better. Since losing weight, I don't really know what I should wear. I shop in Dorothy Perkins and generally buy whatever catches my eye here, which is usually dark colours I can hide behind! I'm usually in jeans.'

Gok got to work. 'I went to get Nicola in a big, pink dress, but her shoulders went up and she didn't like it at all. I thought, I couldn't do this to her,' he said. 'When you're styling someone in such a short period of time, you can't really change their opinion on their body and the way they dress, like I can work on *How To Look Good Naked*. I didn't want to do something she doesn't feel comfortable with and dress her in something she would never wear again.

'She's tall and struggles with clothes but Dorothy Perkins

do amazing long-length trousers, which I put with four-and-a-half-inch heels for a double whammy, as she's lost all this weight. These are perfect for her height and are wide-legged, so hit the widest part of her hip. It's a very classic Chanel-esque look. It's safer than I would have liked, but I didn't have time to convert her. But I think she looks fierce!'

That was also revealing, because it showed that one of the tricks of Gok's success was to spend a great deal of time with each subject, in order to boost their confidence before exploring new types of clothes to wear. Or to put it another way, with Gok it wasn't just about the clothes: it was about a boost in self-esteem and self-confidence. His pep talks to models overcome with nerves on the sets of fashion shoots were legendary, and he was now able to use this technique on ordinary people as well. When he didn't have time to do so, as in this case, he didn't try to push his subject too far, but was still able to use his professional talent to maximise the effect on his subject's appearance.

Gok was often asked who his own style icons were and they were a mixed bunch. 'Katharine Hepburn, I thought she was amazing, and Sophia Loren, I think she was and is still absolutely amazing. Diane Keaton, Dame Judi Dench. I bumped into Judi the other day in Banana Republic, when we were filming the show, and her daughter came up to say how much she loved *Naked*, and I stood there and went [blows raspberry]... I just pooed myself on the floor.

'But I admire her because she's a strong, clever, intelligent, creative woman who dresses impeccably well. Salma Hayek I think looks absolutely amazing. I love Sarah Jessica Parker, I love Patricia Field, I love Vivienne Westwood, I love Alexander McQueen, I love Christopher Kane, there are so many. It's like turning round to Gordon Ramsey and saying, "What's your favourite kind of food?"'

And what of Ramsey himself? Did Gok warm to him? 'Oh my God, yes,' he said. 'A little bit too much. I was speaking about it for about a month. Yeah, he was great. He was loads of fun actually, and I think I intimidated him which was great! Which is what I went in there to do. It was my goal: to go in there and get the little bastard! But he's a lovely guy. Actually, he promised to take me for dinner. He wants to sleep with me.'

And who would Gok like to style? 'Sarah Jessica Parker, because she's always so incredibly well dressed. I'd like to see whether she could get the Gok treatment and it would actually work,' he said. 'I'd really like to do Girls Aloud, just because I'd like to see whether I could do something different that they'd be happy with. They've had a lot of stylists over the years, and I think they'd be quite fun to work with. I've been really lucky because all the people I've really wanted to work with, I've worked with. I know it sounds like I'm blowing my own trumpet now but I've had quite a nice decade of styling, really lucky.'

And what would there be left to do after all that? 'World domination,' was the immediate response. 'I want to sleep with an entire football team… I want to do loads of stuff. I want my own charity — one of the things that I've wanted the whole of my life — and that's becoming more possible now because I think I can throw my name at it, and for all the crap that comes from becoming famous, there's a lot of good you can do.

'That sounds like I'm on a soapbox. It's not meant like that at all, but I've dreamt of having my own charity that I could do support work with. I quite like the idea of standing in front of kids and helping kids. I want to take over the world. I'd love to run for Parliament, I'd like my own shop, I'd love to be a florist. One of the big things is that I want to have kids as well, and that's a full-time job.'

Finally, Gok was asked, what was the first rule of fashion? 'The worst fashion crime is people that wear mobile phones on their belts,' he said. 'It's really wrong, and looks hideous. The best bit of style advice would be to commit to your look, to understand what it is you're doing. If you're going to do the preppy, the yummy mummy, the gothic, the emo, the punk — whatever your look is, commit to it, and understand why you're doing it. Then when anyone points the finger at you and says you look hideous, you can turn and say, "Eff off!" and then you will have absolute justification for how you look.' It was an attitude he applied to his own life, and who could fail to warm to that?

# 15

# WILL THE REAL GOK WAN PLEASE STAND UP?

So who is Gok Wan really? After appearing seemingly out of nowhere to become a phenomenon on our television screens, Gok's rise has been stratospheric. In reality, of course, he is much like the actor who works for years before becoming a sudden, overnight success. Gok laboured long and hard in the shadows before getting where he is today, serving a long, drawn out apprenticeship on any number of television shows before finally getting to front his own.

It was no accident when he finally hit the big time. Television bosses knew exactly what they were getting when they hired Gok. They had worked with him previously, and although no one could have predicted the scale of his forthcoming success, they already knew he was a television natural, with a striking appearance and a personality to go with it. It was an unusual personality as well, for although

Gok still retained the forcefulness he'd cultivated in the overweight years, there was a gentleness about him, too. He could tell women, 'You go, girlfriend!', but he was capable of holding back where necessary, and not going too far.

Above all, as his sister — and to a lesser extent, Gok himself — explained, he had the gift of empathy. He knew what it was to feel he looked horrible. He had cultivated tricks to help him deal with it, and he was capable of passing this experience on to other people. It was telling that he was especially good with damaged women for, underneath it all, Gok was damaged himself. The trauma of his childhood was such that Gok never forgot what it was like to feel the lonely, self-hating outsider, and it was only because he had managed to overcome this ordeal that he blossomed into the man he is today.

But it also fuelled his ambition. Much has been made of his work ethic, not least by Gok himself, and certainly, a good deal of this would have been inherited from his parents. It is no accident that his brother and sister work hard, too. But bullied children are often left with a sense that they will never again allow themselves to be in a position of powerlessness and that throughout the rest of their lives they will show the bullies, and the rest of the world, that they are a person to be stood up to in their own right.

Bullied children frequently become far more successful than anybody could have forecast, for the simple reason that they constantly feel they must prove themselves. No challenge is ever capable of providing the self-worth they need, and so they go on setting themselves ever greater tests. Almost without realising it, this becomes the basis for an extremely successful career. Gok might never have set out to become a famous television presenter – for that is what he is now, however much he still thinks of himself as a stylist – but subconsciously, he almost certainly set out to take on the world and win.

Clearly, Gok has taken to the celebrity lifestyle and all that goes with it with abandon. He is frequently seen at awards ceremonies, star-studded parties and celebrity hangouts like the Groucho Club in London's West End. He fits naturally into the lifestyle: a love of clothes, flamboyance, personality and, of course, success, makes him a natural in the circles in which he now moves.

With fame comes wealth and given how well known his face is these days, he doesn't even need to spend it all on clothes, as he gets given so much, or at least big discounts. Any label would be delighted to see Gok in their clothes: he is a walking advertisement for style, sartorial elegance and flair. It is said that the really lucky turn their hobbies into their careers and Gok has done this with a vengeance. He adores fashion, making him the ideal person to front the shows.

At the same time, Gok has maintained very close links with his family, and even if his increased fame means he doesn't see them as much as he used to, these are ties that will not break. The family all suffered from racial abuse in Leicester, including Gok's parents, and these shared experiences have formed very strong bonds.

But one remarkable result of Gok's fame is that he is, possibly for the first time, truly happy with his mixed racial heritage. Quite apart from anything else, it makes him stand out from a crowd: few Chinese men are as tall as he is, while his Oriental appearance makes him stand out from an Occidental mass. This is another characteristic of bullied children: that while they wish for nothing more than to blend into the crowd when they are young, equally they can be very happy to stand out against it when older. Gok's appearance may have singled him out in a bad way when he was younger, but it has stood him in very good stead as an adult. And the fact that he is now able to explore his Chinese background is an added benefit. Gok has an awareness of the part of the world he could never have cultivated as a child.

Is he really as nice as he seems? On the whole the answer is yes. Given the number of women he's worked with to date, the fact that only one has ever complained about her treatment suggests that Gok really does have a way with women that gives them confidence, and is gentle and kind. The vast majority of the women themselves clearly think so: many are almost embarrassingly effusive in their praise. Gok has actually changed the lives of some of his subjects in a way that has benefited them enormously. The same simply can't be said of the vast majority of makeover shows.

But he clearly has a mischievous side, as well. His language is not for the faint hearted, and he is certainly not above the odd bitchy remark when it comes to the appearance of fellow celebrities. Gok can be catty, not least to entertain those around him. He has a coarser sense of humour than many would expect. But equally, this gives him a down-to-earth quality that makes him far more approachable than someone more aloof. It also puts him at the level of the common man – not some distant fashionista totally lacking the common touch.

Strangely enough, the area that is most closed off to the public view is Gok's private life. Although it is difficult to imagine anyone more openly gay than he is, almost nothing is known about his own romantic history. He might make jokes about wanting to sleep with an entire football team, but when it comes to naming names of actual lovers, he has been entirely discreet. He has never revealed the identity of the Muslim man with whom he shared a seven-year relationship, and nor has any successor ever been publicly spoken about. For all his brashness and openness, the most intimate aspect to his life remains a firmly closed book.

This may be in part because Gok realises that although the British public is very relaxed about homosexuality in many ways, it does not want to shine a light upon the magic. There are very few openly gay couples in British public life today: Sir Elton John and David Furnish are one; George Michael and Kenny Goss are another. But in both cases, the men involved were nothing like as open when they were younger, and were pretty much national treasures by the time they did reveal more about their private lives. And George Michael, rightly or wrongly, believes coming out did actually harm his career. There may be something of that nervousness still at work in Gok.

Or it may just be that he doesn't want to go public with anyone until he's found the right person. As many a celebrity has discovered before him, once you open the door to your private life, it's awfully difficult to shut it again afterwards, when everything has gone wrong. Gok may simply be being cautious with the public, as he once was to his family. And he's certainly open about his wish to meet 'the one'.

In many ways, Gok has also signalled a return to a very different Britain purely through the way that women dress. His approach is totally common sense: start with the basics, control underwear, to give you a silhouette. The last time that approach was used so frequently was in the 1950s, and indeed, Gok frequently refers to that decade when naming his favourite type of look.

The 1950s was a decade when Britain was a very different place. Amid all the uncertainties of the new century, Gok and his acolytes are harking back to a time when British society and values seemed to be stronger than they are now. That was a lost world when Britain emerged triumphant from a war, with a youthful new queen and a future in front of her, not a society that sometimes seemed to have run out of control. Nor is it fanciful to say that Gok himself embodies an older set of virtues. For all the bad language, at the bottom of it all he signifies grace, kindness and charm.

But it is his enormous popularity which is most striking about him, and that looks to continue for many more years.

For Gok has been a revelation. After years of attempting to pull in viewers by being as unpleasant as they could be to their subjects, television makers have suddenly discovered that nice works just as well. In doing so, they have found a figure who gives women back their confidence, who makes them feel better about themselves and whose soaring popularity is testament to the fact that human nature does have a good side. Gok Wan's career looks set flourish for many more years yet.

# Kerry – The Inside Story

## Emily Herbert

Kerry Katona is one of Britain's most talked-about celebrities, juggling the responsibilities of being a dedicated mother with a glamorous front-page lifestyle.

Her tumultuous early childhood saw Kerry witness depression, financial hardship and even a suicide bid by her mother, before being brought up in children's homes and by foster families. Aged just eighteen, however, her fortunes changes and she shot to stardom as one of the founding members of pop group Atomic Kitten, securing a succession of hit singles, sell-out tours and a fairytale wedding – to Westlife's Brian McFadden.

Crowned 'Queen of the Jungle' on *I'm a Celebrity, Get Me Out of Here!* and Celebrity Mum Of The Year in 2004, it looked as though Kerry had left heartache behind for good. But news soon broke that her marriage to Brian was over. Rumours of depression, domestic violence and their break-up filled the papers. Battling the odds once again, she bounced back with a Valentine's Day marriage to Mark Croft and the birth of a beautiful third daughter.

Fully revised to include all the most up-to-date details of Kerry's remarkable and turbulent life, this new edition chronicles her recent falls from grace and her courageous attempts to rise to the top once more.

ISBN 978-1-84454-790-6

**John Blake Publishing Ltd**

# Coming Soon